CULTIVATING JOY IN THE KITCHEN

To Kaline,
Happy Cooking +
Good Health
Love e Vogt

Cultivating Joy in the Kitchen

Plant Forward Recipes & Soulful Nourishment

Cathy Vogt

Cultivating Joy in the Kitchen
Plant-Forward Recipes and Soulful Nourishment

ISBN 1517415624
ISBN 13: 9781517415624
Library of Congress Control Number: 2015915496
CreateSpace Independent Publishing Platform
North Charleston, South Carolina

Printed in the United States of America

To my wonderful husband, who encourages me,
listens to me, tastes all of my creations, and makes me laugh. I love you.

To my beautiful daughters:
You inspire me every day to be a better person.

To my mother and father,
for the gift of this beautiful life and for always
supporting me in following my own path.

CONTENTS

ACKNOWLEDGMENTS

MANY PEOPLE WHOM I have met and worked with along the way have played a part in this book coming together. I thank you.

I am deeply grateful to my mother and father for their encouragement, patience, and love.

I am grateful to my many teachers for the wisdom they have shared: Annemarie Colbin, PhD, and the incredible staff at the Natural Gourmet Institute; the culinary teachers and chefs whom I worked with early in my career. I am thankful for the continuous support of Joshua Rosenthal and the staff at the Institute for Integrative Nutrition™; Marc David and the Institute for the Psychology of Eating™; Sasha Yakovleva and Thomas Fredricksen at The Breathing Center™. I acknowledge and give thanks to Pir Vilayat Inayat Khan and the Abode of the Message; Louise Hay; Smith Farm Center for Healing and the Arts and our many local and organic farmers who work hard every day to ensure we have healthy food to eat.

Thanks to Anne Coleman photography for the last minute photo shoot and lovely authors photo.

I am grateful to each and every client I have worked with over the years who has shared his or her story with me and helped me to learn and grow—as a nutrition coach, a chef, and a person—and to gain a new perspective.

I am thankful to my friends and family for all of the big and little ways they support me.

Mostly, I thank God every day for this life and for being able to do the work that I love.

Introduction

What I have learned from My Kitchen Practice

The kitchen is a place where magic can happen, where simple, perfect ingredients provided by nature can be transformed into delicious meals that fuel our bodies and minds.

Spending time in the kitchen, preparing meals, and learning these skills from our elders were at one time common parts of daily life. Family members of all ages participated in food preparation and shared meals together. A diet of whole, real foods from locally sourced seasonal vegetables, whole grains, and small amounts of high-quality protein, healthy fats, and fruits made up the daily diet. Everything we put into our bodies—the foods we eat and drink, the air we breathe, the thoughts we think—becomes the energy that feeds our cells, ultimately promoting health or contributing to disease.

In today's modern society, most meals are still eaten at home, but we are preparing fewer of them ourselves. People often eat very quickly while engaging in other activities. We are spending less time consciously enjoying our food, as we worry about and rush to whatever is next on the schedule. How many of the meals you eat each week do you pick up from the drive-through window, pop into the microwave, or buy prepackaged from the convenience store? How often does a meal consist of pizza or an energy bar?

Gathering around the table to share a meal is no longer the norm. When we are hungry, we reach for fast, highly processed foods that will give us an energy boost and get us through the day. We are overfed and undernourished, and diet-related diseases are at an all-time high. Our physical bodies need well-balanced foods that make us feel our best. Our minds and spirits also need to be fed—with food that is prepared with love, care, and intention. We know something needs to change but are too busy or too stressed, do not feel well, and do not know where to start.

Wake up, families, women, men, teens, and everyone who eats! Isn't it time to make cooking healthy foods a daily self-care habit? It is time to make peace with the kitchen.

This book will give you a new focus, tips, and simple plant-based recipes that can be adapted to your needs. You can enjoy creating delicious foods that nourish you and bring you joy. This is your life; you are worth it, and you can do it.

With love and in good health,
Cathy Vogt

CHAPTER 1

WHY COOK?

COOKING HEALTHFUL MEALS prepared with real ingredients, whether for family and friends or just for yourself, can be one of the most important daily uses of your time. What we take into our bodies can either offer life-giving nourishment or set us up for disease and ill health. When we lovingly make the space and time to cook, the foods our bodies need, the result is always improved health.

When we eat good food that fits our individual biological needs, we feel good, increase our energy and mental focus, and engage in life in a more meaningful way. Cooking as part of a daily self-care practice is essential.

Cooking can cause frustration and anxiety or it can be a pleasurable, energizing, and creative experience. For those struggling with illness, pain, or depression, it can be a difficult and isolating task. Getting the right balance of nutrients can be a powerful means of helping the body heal and repair. A meal created with love can encourage those who struggle with illness to accept the support of those around them and to experience strength from loving, human connections.

My relationship with cooking began with a strong impulse to create something that made the people around me happy. As a teenager, I learned how to transform simple ingredients into meals as a way to help when my mother returned to work. I quickly moved from Hamburger Helper to learning basic skills from a cookbook I received for my thirteenth birthday. I enjoyed the challenge of trying something new and

1

presenting it to the people; I loved, even though I did not always view it as a success. Accepting my mishaps and being open to the opportunity to learn and grow came much later.

During my formal culinary training, and in the many professional kitchens where I have worked, I learned to hone my knife skills, to master basic cooking techniques, and to work quickly and efficiently, moving effortlessly around others as in a well-rehearsed dance. I learned how to cook while running from one task to another and left the kitchen at the end of my shift very exhausted. Cooking in a professional kitchen can be a rewarding and creative activity. A good kitchen crew can be like a family: supportive, challenging, encouraging, and, sometimes, frustrating. The staff of a well-run kitchen is completely focused on delivering to their guests an amazing meal and experience. I have been lucky to be a part of many great kitchen crews.

I acquired a deep level of learning and awareness during my apprenticeship at a spiritual center in upstate New York. I made whole-grain breads using yeast that we placed in large bowls to rise in the sun in the courtyard. We harvested Herbs and vegetables daily from the community garden. I learned how to grow sprouts and to put away foods for the winter in the outdoor canning kitchen.

In the spiritual center kitchen, cooking was a community event where all those preparing the meal began by joining hands for a moment of silence. Giving attention to the importance and sacredness of preparing a meal is something that I have continued to practice each time I cook. The colors of the vegetables we harvested were vibrant and vivid. We grew alfalfa, broccoli, radishes, mung beans, and other sprouts year-round. Spontaneous singing was common, and meals were family style. People ate slowly and lingered over conversation. I left the kitchen at the end of mealtime feeling joyful and fulfilled.

Cooking for myself and for others has given me a way to connect easily in a larger community. I have witnessed the healing power that a homemade meal can have for someone who is feeling disconnected, alone, overwhelmed, discouraged, or ill. This simple and powerful gesture can result in a wave of positive change. Celebrating and sharing a meal with a larger community fills a deeper need that calories alone cannot touch. Food, which is healthy and alive with life energy, can be a great connector, healer and teacher.

An important part of my daily life is cooking for my own family, clients, and friends. Cooking is a life skill that has taught me many lessons: how to, have patience, develop trust, let go, accept help, laugh more, and let in all of the goodness that life has to offer.

The practice of cooking can create a centering space in an overly busy world.

Teaching yourself and your children how to prepare healthy meals is a gift that should be shared and embraced. When we know how and what to feed ourselves without relying on someone else to do it, we step into a place of clarity and power in our lives.

NOURISHMENT PRACTICE

How can home-cooked foods change your health and your relationships with yourself and others? Jot down any thoughts that come up.

Positive Thoughts
I take care of my own health, so I choose to cook and prepare foods that are best for me.

CHAPTER 2

YES, YOU CAN! GET OFF THE COUCH AND INTO THE KITCHEN

DECIDING HOW WE spend our time each day sometimes feels like it is out of our control. As a society, we are busy juggling work, relationships, daily responsibilities; finding time to exercise; and trying to relax to relieve stress. Multitasking is the norm, and getting into the kitchen before we have even thought about cooking can be an overwhelming idea. If you feel that watching cooking shows has replaced actual time in the kitchen preparing meals, you are not alone. It is time to rethink what is really going on. Are you finding more reasons to stay out of the kitchen and rely on grab-and-go processed foods, drive-through, and takeout? Do your meals often consist of something that comes out of a box, dry cereal and milk in a bowl, or other convenience foods that deplete your energy? How is this approach working for you?

Where you are in your journey is OK—no judgments. Lovingly acknowledge any resistance you may be feeling or negative thoughts you may be having. Negative thinking can stall us in our attempts to take action for our own betterment. How can you step into the kitchen and start creating better health? There is a place in the kitchen for everyone.

One couple I worked with wanted to eat better and get out of the takeout-foods-for-dinner rut. They were both professionals who had very demanding schedules that did not leave much time to spend together. Instead of making a complicated meal, they started to create simple salad-based meals together—chopping lettuce and adding different kinds of vegetables, leftovers, beans, and hard-boiled eggs to create a beautiful meal. They looked forward to this evening routine. They relaxed, laughed, turned off their electronic devices, and turned on music they enjoyed. For this couple, making salad dinners together strengthened their relationship and improved their health and energy.

Nourishment Practice

Spend five to ten minutes upon waking and five to ten minutes before going to sleep to observe your thinking. Let your thoughts flow naturally. Notice when your mind wanders to that worrying, anxious, and negative space. Have a pad of paper and pen ready, and write down what comes up (even if it does not seem to make any sense). Gently acknowledge your thoughts and then let them go. Much of our thinking is a learned habit that we can change. Can your negative thoughts be replaced with thinking that supports you in a loving and kind way?

Try practicing this exercise for two weeks and see what changes you notice. Continue to replace negative thoughts with positive thinking, and move toward taking action.

Positive Thoughts
I acknowledge my negative thoughts and lovingly replace them with gentle, empowered thinking.

I Have No Time to Cook or I'm Too Stressed

The most common reason clients give for not cooking is, "I have no time." How we manage our time each day is a series of active choices. Do thoughts of not having enough time or an endless list of obligations make you feel anxious and stressed? What do you think you have time for in your life? Is preparing healthy meals a priority?

When asked, most people will admit to feeling that they are overwhelmed, too busy, and do not have enough time to accomplish everything they feel they need to each day. Does this sound familiar to you?

When we experience any real or imagined stressors in our lives, our bodies respond with many physiological reactions, including increased heart rate, rapid breathing, increased blood pressure, and difficulty focusing. Stress compromises metabolism, nutrient absorption, and immune function. Living in a constant state of stress and anxiety, even at a low level, can have a great impact on how we function on a day-to-day basis.

I learned how my constant, unhealthy and rapid breathing was affecting my health, when my chronic asthma condition spiraled out of control and left me unable to sleep or to function. I discovered the Breathing Center and Dr. K. P. Buteyko's work. With the support and training of Breathing Normalization specialists Thomas Fredrickson and Sasha Yakovleva at the Breathing Center, I relearned how to breathe in a natural and healthy way and began to rebuild my health. Constant low levels of anxiety that had been present for many years disappeared; I spent less time worrying and felt an inner sense of peace. When we slow down and reduce our breathing, we reduce our stress.

The following two excerpts, which are taken from The Breathingcenter.com website, express the importance of healthy breathing and explain how to use breathing exercises to help reduce stress.

"Reduced breathing makes the nervous system healthier and less reactive. People who normalize their breathing always become calmer, more balanced, and emotionally less vulnerable."

"This discovery was made sixty years ago by a renowned Russian scientist, K. P. Buteyko, MD. He realized that breathing affects health more than eating and drinking. Why? Without food, we can survive for weeks; without water, for days; without air, only a few minutes. Air is as powerful as nuclear energy, capable of destroying or restoring health very quickly. Dr. Buteyko said that everyone who over breathes creates Chernobyl in their own bodies. Learning how to breathe less reestablishes the natural balance in the body, which is called 'health.'"

For many people, lifestyle factors play an important role in how their bodies function. Rushing through the activities of each day has become normal. When we slow down and remove the obstacles that cause our bodies to function in a constant state of stress, time opens up and it becomes easier to focus.

How you organize, your time can greatly affect your perceived level of stress. Is there time allotted in your daily routine for preparing a meal? Do you like breaking things down into small chunks, or do you prefer spending a larger block of time on accomplishing a task? Start by scheduling a day and time to make a simple list of the tasks involved in preparing meals. Having a plan sets you up for success and ensures that you have the ingredients you need when you start cooking.

Fifteen to twenty minutes of planning and preparation can make the difference between eating breakfast each morning, or skipping it and making poor food choices all day long. If you are a busy parent with children, getting everyone ready each morning can be overwhelming. Look at the breakfast recipe section for some ideas to get you started.

NOURISHMENT PRACTICE

Try taking a few minutes to slow down; clear a space in your mind to consider the possibility of trying something new. Sit down with your feet firmly on the floor (take off your shoes, if possible), and adjust your posture so you are sitting up straight. Relax your shoulders and arms, and place your hands in your lap. Notice your breathing: is it fast or slow? Be an observer. Are you breathing through your mouth or your nose? If you are breathing through your mouth, close your mouth and switch to nasal breathing. Close your eyes and gently begin to slow down your breathing. Inhale slowly through your nose, and let yourself exhale naturally; do this at a pace that is comfortable for you. Focus on slow breathing for several minutes until it feels relaxed, easy, and satisfying. Notice the natural pause of your breath after you exhale. Take a few minutes each day to practice slowing down your breathing, and notice how you feel afterward.

Positive Thoughts
I use my time wisely and have all the time I need to prepare healthy meals.

INCREASE YOUR ENERGY

Is low energy preventing you from getting into a regular kitchen routine?

An underlying health issue, food sensitivities, dehydration, nutritional deficiencies, lack of sleep, depression, or the side effects of medication can all result in low energy. It is important to identify what the core issues are and to follow a healing strategy to address them.

Self-defeating thinking will drain your energy, too. Continue to remind yourself to change your thoughts to those that are peaceful, loving, and gentle. Take cooking off the chore or to-do lists in your mind, and move it to the list of gifts you give yourself.

Are you a morning person or an evening person? Take advantage of the times of the day when you have high energy to do some planning and prep work for upcoming meals. One of my clients got creative with the time she spends waiting to pick up her children at sports events. She keeps a bag of food magazines and cookbooks in her car, plans menus, and makes lists while she waits. She told me that this has become one of her most relaxing activities. She disconnects from her electronic devices, thumbs leisurely through magazines with beautiful pictures, and creates a healthful meal plan and her shopping lists.

NOURISHMENT PRACTICE

When your energy is low, try these simple steps:

Hydrate—slowly drink a glass of clean water. Pay attention to how it feels and how your body responds. Pour another glass and sip it slowly. When is the last time you had a drink of water?

Get up and move your body. Take a break to stretch, go for a walk, do a short yoga practice, turn on some music and dance, or engage in another exercise that gets your body moving.

When is the last time you had something to eat, and what was it? Make time for balanced meals to maintain consistent, high energy levels.

Positive Thoughts
I have all the energy I need to create the life I want.

SKILLS: I DON'T KNOW HOW TO COOK

Knowing how to prepare a meal that is nutritionally balanced and tasty is not common knowledge; it requires a series of skills that can be learned. Many adult clients with whom I have spoken were not allowed in the kitchen to experiment with cooking while they were growing up. They were told it was too messy, too dangerous, or unimportant. For some people, being in the kitchen can feel like a foreign land that is confusing and unfamiliar.

The good news about cooking skills is that you can dive in and learn them at any age. Families, partners, and children can do this by choosing a simple meal to prepare together. There are many resources available to help you learn the basic skills of cooking. These include libraries, community centers, local and online cooking classes, cookbooks, or even a skilled friend. Be curious and open to trying new foods. Cooking can be as simple as slicing an avocado and stuffing it with a delicious salad, blending a smoothie, or making a three-course meal; it is up to you.

NOURISHMENT PRACTICE

Make a list of one or two new recipes or cooking techniques that you want to focus on this week. Write it down, and plan when you are going to buy the ingredients you need so they are available. Pick a day you are going to prepare it where you don't feel rushed.

Positive Thoughts
I am open and receptive to learning and improving my skills in the kitchen.

SUPPORT: WHAT KIND OF SUPPORT FEELS RIGHT FOR YOU?

Does cooking a meal for yourself or your family feel like a big task that you do not even want to start? Do not let your thoughts overwhelm you before you get started.

You can lovingly create the support you need to simplify the experience. Enlist a cooking friend to spend a few hours with you on a weekend or a day off to prep meals that can be frozen or reheated. Enjoy the company of someone you do not often get to see and create beautiful food together.

Divide the tasks involved in preparing a meal with other family members; even the smallest child can tear salad greens or wash vegetables. If you have older teenagers, ask them to plan and prepare a family meal. If illness is preventing you from cooking meals, please ask for assistance. Friends and family want to help but often do not know how. Preparing a meal is a wonderful gift that nourishes both the giver and the receiver. Do not be shy about letting the person doing the cooking know if certain foods are off limits. Share a few simple recipes that someone can prepare that are healing for you at the time. Focus on nutrient dense, simple meals such as vegetable based broths, bone broths and easy to digest soups when you are recovering from illness. These types of foods are easy to prepare in large quantities and can be frozen in individual sized portions.

NOURISHMENT PRACTICE

List the actions you will take this week to find the support you need in the kitchen.

Positive Thoughts
I ask for and receive the positive support I need.

IT'S TOO MESSY

I have worked with many people who have gorgeous, spotless kitchens that never get messy. Is the idea of a dirty, unorganized kitchen keeping you from cooking? Life itself is often messy and a little disorganized and needs to be tidied up occasionally. On the other hand, if your kitchen space looks more like the all-purpose room, the home office, a mail drop-off spot, or a homework or craft area, it is time to reclaim it and start fresh. Pick a one- to two-hour window of time, roll up your sleeves, and do some serious straightening up. Preparing each meal in a clean and inviting space opens up more possibilities for enjoying the process.

To get started, pick one-pot meals that require minimal clean up and invest in a few timesaving tools for your kitchen. Being creative can be messy, but it is an investment worthy of your time and attention. Music that inspires and uplifts you can be a good motivator to get started and a good companion when it comes time to clean up.

NOURISHMENT PRACTICE

Make a list of simple one-pot meals or meals that you can create using ingredients that you already have.

Positive Thoughts
I enjoy cleaning my kitchen and making space to create a delicious and nourishing meal whenever I choose.

CHAPTER 3

CHANGE YOUR RELATIONSHIP: FIND YOUR INSPIRATION

HAVE YOU EVER been in a relationship that drained your energy and left you feeling anxious, stressed, or physically ill? The relationship may have started out being supportive and positive but now is no longer working, and you know something needs to change. Taking a step into unknown territory can be a fear that prevents us from moving forward to something better. Many of us are more comfortable with the status quo even if it's just not working anymore; at least it is known, and there is some sense of security in that.

Do not be fooled by this thinking. Be willing to let go of old eating habits, food choices that compromise your health and thoughts that no longer serve you. Open up your mind to new possibilities one-step at a time. What could your life look like if you decided to change your thinking and started cooking healthier foods?

Visualize Your Best Life

When our lives are overly busy every day, it is hard to imagine that there is the space or energy for change to happen. Sometimes we get caught up in those around us who seem to run from one activity to another. I remember as a young child one of my favorite activities in the summer was lying in the grass, gazing at the clouds floating by overhead. I spent many hours involved in this activity, and I can still recall the feeling of peace and well-being it gave me.

As an adult, I went through a very difficult year dealing with a chronic and debilitating health issue that required me to slow down. I spent many winter days focused on relaxation and healthy breathing exercises while watching the squirrels build a nest high up in the trees. This practice reminded me that being still and quiet was just as important to my overall health as taking action.

When is the last time you turned down the noise in your mind to daydream?

Many people find a structured practice such as yoga, meditation, walking, or chanting to be beneficial. Find something you enjoy that you can practice on a regular basis. Regularly engaging in a mindfulness practice brings a mental clarity that can lead to positive action.

Nourishment Practice

Find a quiet space, preferably outdoors in nature where you feel relaxed and comfortable, and visualize yourself happy and healthy. What do you look like and how do you feel? Notice anything that stands out or any sensations that you have and jot them down. Start with ten to fifteen minutes daily and increase gradually at your own comfort level. Clearly see the life you desire.

Positive Thoughts
I am the loving creator of my life.

Beauty and Real Foods

What kinds of foods fuel your body with exactly what you need?

Real foods found in nature are inspiring in their unique beauty. Foods that are healthy, fresh, and alive have a vibrant quality; their colors are deep and rich. Have you ever really looked at a freshly picked, ripe tomato or strawberry? The shapes and patterns of natural foods are exquisite and visually appealing. Our senses of smell and taste allow us to relish and enjoy flavor profiles, such as salty, sweet, sour, and bitter.

Real foods provide a complete and perfectly balanced package of flavor, fiber, and nutrients that our bodies are designed to eat and enjoy. Always choose real food first.

Combine a few foods with different flavor profiles together and you have a completely new taste sensation. Try a slice of ripe melon, next add a sprinkle of cinnamon, and then lime juice. How does that taste? Have you ever experienced the enjoyment of eating a fresh tomato right off the vine or the flavor and texture of an apple eaten in an orchard? What is appealing to you? Be willing to add in new, whole foods that you have never had before; you just may discover something wonderful.

Bring a little bit of nature into your kitchen. Place a few pots of fresh herbs on your kitchen windowsill or fill up a pretty bowl with seasonal fruits. Place crystals and beautiful stones that you have gathered in a sunny spot to catch the light that comes in through a nearby window. Add some sprigs of basil or parsley to your flower bouquet. Make a batch of fruit-and-mint iced tea and pour it into a jar or pitcher so it is the first thing you see when you look inside your refrigerator.

One of my single female clients was working hard at adopting new and nourishing eating habits. She set aside a small amount of her weekly food budget to purchase a beautiful bouquet of flowers each week.

She placed the arrangement in a vintage crystal vase that was a gift from her mother. The flowers were set on a small table at the entrance to her kitchen where she was greeted with their beautiful and exquisite colors and fragrance each time she entered.

Hang up a photograph or painting in your kitchen that makes you smile when you look at it. Let your first experience of entering your kitchen space be one of beauty that supports your happiness. We are naturally drawn to things that are beautiful, so surround yourself with that which inspires.

Have you ever noticed that the visual appeal of processed food is all in the packaging? Manufacturing companies employ chemical engineers who are experts at combining different flavor profiles in the laboratory to make their products irresistible. There are many processed foods are made with whole, real, and high-quality ingredients; be very selective when choosing. Learn to read food-product labels like a detective. Know what you are eating. These should be a very small part of your weekly meals.

Nourishment Practice

Look around your kitchen space and notice how you feel. Does the space draw you in or make you want to head out the door? What small changes can you make so it is more appealing to you? Write down a list.

On your next grocery-shopping trip try out a different approach. Choose a different shopping venue. If you normally do your shopping at the grocery store or convenience store, search out a local farm stand or market that sells local produce. Notice the foods that appeal to you;

beautiful colors, interesting shapes and use these as a starting point for your meal. Pick something new.

Positive Thoughts
I deserve the best nutrition, and I choose whole, real foods that I enjoy.

SIMPLICITY IS BEST

I love to cook and create plant-focused meals to serve to my clients and family. Plant-based foods are easier to digest and assimilate. Many people today suffer from a wide range of digestive and diet-related disorders, such as irritable bowel syndrome, colitis, gastro-esophageal reflux disease, celiac disease, autoimmune diseases, heart disease, and diabetes.

How does your body feel after a large holiday meal that includes many different types of food and that is more than your body needs? It can become an endless cycle of too much, and our bodies are not designed to handle that.

Simplify the foods and number of different ingredients you serve during each meal, and give your body and your digestion a break. Eating a wide variety of natural foods is great, but you do not have to eat them all in one meal. Focus on the quality of ingredients when preparing food and not the quantity of dishes you prepare.

Invest what your budget allows in organic and locally sourced ingredients. Design your meals around what is in season where you live, and check local markets and farms. Young children, when given the choice, will pick simple, whole-ingredient meals: hard-boiled eggs; nuts; fresh green beans; and slices of tomato, cucumber, and carrot. Planning meals can be a lot easier and less stressful with this approach. Unfortunately, many of us find this type of meal unappealing and find the flavor of whole foods tasteless. Maybe it is time to reintroduce our palate to the flavors of real food. Supermarket shopping becomes much easier when you only have to shop in a few areas of the store.

Look at the Recipes section and the **Pairings Guides** throughout Chapter nine to turn a simple recipe into a complete meal.

Nourishment Practice

Pick two or three fresh whole food, plant based ingredients, and design your meal around them. See what is in your refrigerator and pantry right now, and come up with a meal. Keep it simple.

Positive Thoughts
I take loving care of my body and feed it simple, well-balanced meals.

Health and Vitality

There is nothing more valuable and appealing than vibrant health. Diet and lifestyle choices—poor quality processed food, smoking, excessive alcohol consumption, a sedentary lifestyle, and stress—are key factors in many chronic health conditions. If you are struggling with health issues, do not let yourself be defeated by negative, self-destructive thinking. When we live with a chronic health condition over a long period, it becomes difficult to remember what it felt like to be pain-free, energized, and physically and emotionally healthy. Let go of the internal conflict and self-criticism that can keep you stuck. Allow yourself to stop the waiting and let your life begin now! You are not your illness or your condition.

Be present and take control over the choices you make to support your healing process. Food changes everything. Replace health-depleting foods, refined sugars, processed foods, artificial sweeteners and low quality and damaged fats with fresh, life-promoting, and healing foods. Seek out the information and answers that will move you into a place of empowered thinking and action. Be consistently persistent in taking small steps and making positive changes.

Nourishment Practice

Make a list of two to three simple things that will move you in the direction of better health but that you have not started yet. Start with something that is easy for you to do right now, and see how you feel after one to two weeks of consistency. Celebrate your success.

Positive Thoughts
I am healthy; I am strong; I am happy; I am whole.

CHAPTER 4

MAKE YOUR KITCHEN A PLACE YOU LOVE TO BE

HAVING A WELL-ORGANIZED kitchen stocked with the basic tools and ingredients makes the journey to healthful eating a lot more enjoyable. Enjoying your kitchen space does not mean having the largest space, the most expensive equipment, or a pantry that looks like the inside of a gourmet grocery store.

I have cooked in many types of kitchens: a tiny apartment kitchen with a two-foot butcher-block counter, brand-new commercial hotel kitchens, a summer camp with no refrigerator and portable gas stoves, and more. Sometimes it is the little quirks and organizational aspects of your kitchen space that make you feel defeated. Is this type of thinking that you use as an excuse not to cook?

I remember one of my clients who hated to cook and avoided her kitchen. One day I received a call from her, and she excitedly shared a realization. She said, "I am short, and everything in my kitchen is set up for someone much taller (my husband). However, I am the one who does most of the cooking. I have to stretch and get on a step stool to get down anything I need from my cabinets just to get started, and it's so frustrating." She spent an afternoon reorganizing her kitchen so that what she needed was within easy reach.

Another one of my clients realized that everything in his kitchen was set up for someone who was right-handed. He was left-handed and the flow never really felt right.

Look around your kitchen. Are there a few easy things that you could change right now that would help you feel more at ease? Are your knives and cooking utensils easily accessible? Is it convenient and safe for you to take out heavier objects such as pots, pans, and bowls when you need them? Are the spices and seasonings that you use on a daily basis right where you need them? I keep a small tray with my favorite ones right near the stove and others nearby in a drawer.

NOURISHMENT PRACTICE
Make a list of a few changes that you need to make in your kitchen. Write down the date when you are going to take action. Start with something simple.

Positive Thoughts
I organize my kitchen in a way that works well for me.

SOMETHING MY GRANDMOTHER USED IN HER KITCHEN

Have you ever heard of the kitchen referred to as the heart of the home? The kitchen can be the place where you, your family, and your friends are well fed in body, mind, and spirit.

When I was growing up, my family did not have a lot of extra money many of our meals included whatever ingredients were available from our garden. Our tiny apartment kitchen was a place where friends stopped in for a cup of tea or to share a meal that was offered by my mother. I remember family events with my aunt, uncle, and grandparents sitting around the kitchen table sharing a meal and me, soaking in the love.

I remember the first apartment I lived in after graduating from college, when I moved to a new city. I saved my money to purchase my first good set of cookware in which I created many wonderful meals and memories that I shared with new friends. Many of my friends at that time worked in hotels, and many of us had Mondays off. We regularly gathered on Monday evening—cooking, laughing, and sharing foods from our diverse cultural backgrounds.

There are rituals that live within each of us—meals served in a special dish, the tablecloth used only on birthdays, and the knife that my father used to carve the holiday turkey.

In addition to these physical objects, we each have memories of cooking and sharing foods that connect us to people who are important in our lives. Maybe those nourishing memories are of special friends, community, or part of a certain time in your life. You can choose to focus on the memories that bring you joy and carry them forward into your present day. If you are lucky enough to have that special dish, carving knife, or the birthday tablecloth, take it out and use it.

Is there a special ritual or object associated l with cooking and sharing food that is meaningful to you?

NOURISHMENT PRACTICE

Make a list of your memories about food, rituals, special dishes, and traditions. Cross out those that you are ready to let go of and no longer bring you joy and incorporate new ideas that support you in your present life.

Positive Thoughts
I am thankful for the traditions that bring joy to my life.

JOYFUL KITCHEN ESSENTIALS

Having the basic tools like pans, small wares, and sharpened kitchen knives makes cooking more joyful and comfortable. Below is a list of some of the essentials; feel free to add items as you need to. Yard sales, swaps, consignment stores, online sources, and generous friends are a great way to stock your kitchen space inexpensively.

Ladle: Choose one with a hooked end, which is convenient for hanging. Various sizes are available: 2 ounce, 4 ounce, 6 ounce, etc.

Metal Tongs: These are my most used kitchen tool. Use tongs to pick up, mix, and turn foods over. Locking tongs are the easiest to use and to store away. Look for ones with scalloped edges.

Metal Spatula: Use this to turn foods over in a sauté pan, to flip pancakes, etc.

Rubber Spatula: Scrape out bowls and containers with this tool.

Metal Wire Whisk or Balloon Whisk: Look for one that is sturdy, with the handle and whisk attachment firmly attached and a comfortable handle.

Assorted Wooden Spoons, Metal Spoons, and Slotted Metal Spoons: Mix ingredients and remove food from liquids with these tools.

Metal Box Grater: Choose one that has four sides. Use it to grate everything from hard cheese and carrots to onions and chocolate. Look for one with a comfortable rubber handle.

Nut-Milk Bag: Use this fine-mesh cloth or nylon bag to strain nut milks and to strain vegetables and fruit purees.

Micro Plane: Use to grate and zest citrus fruits, cheese and chocolate with this handheld tool.

Vegetable Peeler: V-shaped models are more versatile than those with the traditional swivel head are are. Look for one with a comfortable rubber handle.

Can Opener: Use to open assorted-sized cans; the handheld type is fine.

Pastry Brush: Baste, brush egg washes onto foods, apply oil, etc. with this tool.

Garlic Press: Many are not dishwasher-safe. Look for one that is easy to clean.

Measuring Spoons: The best option is a metal set that has increments of ¼ teaspoon, ½ teaspoon, 1 teaspoon, and 1 tablespoon.

Dry Measuring-Cup Set: Again, the best choice is a metal set that has a capacity of ¼ cup, ⅓ cup, ½ cup, and 1 cup.

Liquid Measuring Cup: Choose one that is made of glass and that holds one cup or two cups.

Kitchen Shears: Invest in ones with fine, serrated tips. Look for ones that have comfortable rubber handles.

Instant-Read Thermometer: Select one with a metal stem and a glass head; do not leave this tool in the oven.

Paring Knife/Chef Knife/Serrated Slicing Knife: When purchasing kitchen knives, look for high-carbon stainless steel with a comfortable handle. Always hold a knife in your hand to see if it is comfortable for you before purchasing.

Sharpening or honing Steel: A rod of steel, ceramic or diamond coated steel, used to realign the knife blade edges.

Sharpening Stone or Electric Knife Sharpener: This tool will put an edge back on your knives. Many stores that sell high-quality knives offer knife-sharpening services.

Citrus Juicer: Choose a handheld type for juicing lemons and lime. There are several good options, including a wooden reamer, an old-fashioned glass type, or one in which you place a lemon half and squeeze with a strainer. You can also successfully juice a lemon, lime, or orange by cutting it in half and squeezing it by hand.

Pepper Mill or Spice Grinder: Use this to grind fresh peppercorns, sesame seeds, flax seeds

Fine Wire Mesh Colander: This is convenient for washing grains that would otherwise fall through a regular-sized colander.

Colander: Use to drain and wash vegetables, beans, grains, pasta, etc.

Salad Spinner: Use to wash leafy greens and fresh herbs.

Cutting Boards: There is a variety to choose from; wooden boards are lovely. Choose those made of plastic or recycled composite materials, which can be washed and sanitized in the dishwasher. Always have at least two cutting boards. Use one for raw meats, fish, and poultry only to prevent cross-contamination between raw and cooked foods. Color-coded cutting boards are available for easy designation.

Assorted Mixing-Bowl Set: Generally there are four sizes to a set; I prefer glass or pottery-style bowls, but these are heavier to lift than stainless steel. Some bowls have lids that fit on top for storage purposes.

Steamer Basket: Choose one that is made of metal or bamboo and that fits into your pots.

Sauté pan: Purchase two sizes: small (8 inch) and large (10 inch to 12 inch).

Various-Size Pots with Lids: Select small (1 quart to 2 quart) and large (5 quart, 7 quart, or 10 quart) sizes. I recommend high quality stainless steel with an aluminum or copper core for better heat distribution and resistance to rust and corrosion.

I recommend that you avoid the use of aluminum and nonstick cookware. Aluminum is toxic, and nonstick cookware can release toxic gases during cooking. They can also easily pit and chip, introducing toxic metals into your foods. See the Resource page for safe cookware brands.

Small Wares and Time Savers to Consider:

Food Processor: Buy one with a good motor. S-shaped, metal cutting blades and shredding discs are very helpful and time saving.

Roasting Pan/Sheet Pans: Invest in well-made pans that will not warp in the oven.

Hand Blender: An immersion-style blender is perfect for using directly in a pot; it usually comes with a whisk-style attachment.

Wok: Use this tool for making high-heat, stir-fry dishes; poaching; and other tasks.

High-Speed Blender: I prefer a transparent container. It is easy to see the contents, and it does not get as hot as a stainless steel container when blending hot liquids. Vitamix, Ninja, and Kitchen Aid are all good blenders that you can purchase at various price points. Shop around for the one that fits your needs best; many have additional-sized blender bowls that fit onto the base.

Cast-Iron Griddle: This fits over two burners on the stovetop; one side is flat (perfect for searing and making pancakes, sandwiches.), and the other side has ridges on it (great for grilling vegetables).

JOYFUL KITCHEN: PANTRY ESSENTIALS

Organizing and stocking your kitchen pantry with healthy ingredients makes it easy to create a delicious meal quickly. Plant-Based Foods+Pantry Essentials+Protein=Happy Eating.

A WORD ABOUT SALT

High-quality salt is one of the most important ingredients for health and flavor in any kitchen. Avoid commercial salt; it is bleached and chemically produced and has no nutritional value. Although commercial salt is cheap, it cannot compare to sea salt or to salt mined from the earth and sun dried. Both of these contain an abundance of trace minerals and iodine that our bodies easily assimilate. High-quality brands of salt, harvested by hand, increases the cost. Make sure the salt you choose comes from a clean, unpolluted source.

Real salt is necessary for overall health and functioning of all of bodily fluids, nerves, and cells. Do a taste test of commercial salt and quality salt and notice the flavor difference. Real salt has a mellow, sometimes sweet, flavor and a variety of nuances. Commercial salt has a metallic flavor and a chemical aftertaste. Invest in real salt for cooking, and use the commercial salt for cleaning.

MY FAVORITE SESAME SEED CONDIMENT

Gomasio is a condiment I discovered years ago and has priority placement right next to my Himalayan salt and pepper grinder. Gomasio is a Japanese condiment popular in macrobiotic cooking, made with toasted ground sesame seeds and salt (Himalayan salt/sea salt). Sesame seeds are a good source of calcium and add a nice nutty flavor to savory foods. Toast 1 cup of raw sesame seeds on top of the stove in a small skillet until lightly browned, add 1-Tablespoon salt and cook for a minute longer, (be careful not to burn them). Grind seeds/salt mixture in blender for

20-30 seconds until coarsely ground. Alternately, you can store gomasio mixture in a small handheld spice grinder and grind it, as you need it. Optional ingredients: dulse, dried herbs, garlic granules, hemp seeds, cumin, peppercorns or other flavorings.

Herbs and Spices
_____Basil
_____Oregano
_____Thyme
_____Chili Powder
_____Bay Leaves
_____Curry Powder
_____Turmeric
_____Dry Mustard
_____Peppercorns
_____Cumin
_____Paprika
_____Crushed Red Pepper
_____Sea Vegetable Shake
_____Garlic, ground
_____Ginger, ground

Nuts and Seeds
_____Raw Almonds, (whole/ ground)
_____Raw Walnuts
_____Raw Cashews
_____Raw Pumpkin Seeds
_____Raw Sunflower Seeds
_____Hemp Seeds
_____Chia Seeds
_____Coconut (Shredded/ Flakes)
_____Sesame Seeds
_____Flaxseed
_____Hazelnuts

Fats and Oils
_____Olive Oil
_____Extra-Virgin Olive Oil
_____Coconut Oil (refined/ unrefined)
_____Sesame Oil
_____Toasted Sesame Oil

Vinegars and Seasonings
_____Raw Apple-Cider Vinegar
_____Aged Balsamic Vinegar
_____Brown-Rice Vinegar
_____Umeboshi Plum Vinegar
_____Lemon Juice, Lime Juice
_____Coconut Vinegar
_____Naturally Fermented Tamari
_____Coconut Aminos
_____Hot Sauce or Siracha

Cans and Jars
_____Tomato Paste
_____Coconut Milk
_____Coconut Cream
_____Mustard, (Dijon/yellow)
_____Capers
_____Tahini
_____Almond Butter
_____Whole Peeled Tomatoes
_____Artichoke Hearts
_____Salsa

Beans and Legumes
_____Lentils (red/brown/green)
_____Black Beans
_____Chickpeas
_____Beans (heirloom varieties)
_____Split Peas
_____Pinto Beans

Whole Grains
_____Brown Rice (long grain/
short)
_____Basmati Rice
_____Oats, (rolled/steel cut)
_____Millet
_____Quinoa
_____Buckwheat kasha

Sweeteners
_____Raw Honey
_____Xylitol
_____Stevia Liquid
_____Maple Syrup
_____Dried Fruit (Apricots,
Cranberries, Dates, Figs,
Cherries)
_____Raw Cacao (Powder/nibs)
_____Chocolate (organic/
70% cocoa)

Other Important Stuff
_____Aluminum-Free Baking
Powder
_____Arrowroot Powder

_____Baking Soda
_____Kudzu/ Kuzu
_____Nori Sheets
_____Arame
_____Wakame
_____Kombu
_____Dulse
_____Dried Mushrooms
_____Miso

CHAPTER 5

DISCOVER YOUR COOKING STYLE

WE ARE ALL unique and different. Each of us has their own way of doing things that makes sense and feels right. Find a kitchen style that suits you best. As life flows and is constantly changing, you may find that your cooking style evolves as you become more comfortable and learn new skills.

FOLLOW THE RECIPE

Well-written recipes give clear, concise steps and directions and should be easy to follow, even if you have never made a particular dish before. Reading a recipe all the way through before, starting the process of cooking is important. It allows you to access important information, such as: the amount of time needed to prepare and cook the dish, how to prepare the ingredients, the processes involved and the equipment needed, what needs to be set up, special handling of ingredients, and a mental picture of how the dish will look when it is done. Even if you have made something similar before, resist the urge to jump right in before reading the instructions so you do not miss something important. There are many different ways to use the same ingredients, and variations can greatly change the final dish.

I remember fondly a participant who came to many of my cooking classes. She enjoyed the social aspects of the class and loved trying new foods. Most of the recipes she prepared did not turn out as intended, and she was always quite puzzled. While chatting with friends she had not seen in a while, she would quickly gather the ingredients, chop, mix, stir, and look at the recipe occasionally as she went along. Does this sound like you? It is very common, but you may be missing an important part of the process by not reading the recipe first.

Read through and follow the recipe the first time you prepare it. After trying a recipe for the first time, feel free to customize it to your liking.

Following a recipe is like having a personal cooking guide right in the kitchen. Read the recipe, and jot down notes to help you remember important steps. I have written and read hundreds of recipes from many different areas of the world, and I am still discovering new techniques and gems of wisdom.

Recipes are not a required to prepare a meal. If you tend to be intuitive or creative, or just enjoy doing your own thing, improvising is a great way to explore and be a little playful in the kitchen. To get started, pick a few ingredients that excite you and decide on a cooking technique, such as sautéed, pan-fried, or baked or raw-food preparation. Consider the season and the weather to help determine what might work best. If you are knowledgeable about basic preparation and methods, this can be a very enjoyable process and an exercise in letting go of perfection.

I clearly remember baking a birthday cake for my mother when I was a teenager. I had just recently discovered how much I liked to cook, and my mother was very generous in allowing me to use the kitchen as my laboratory. I found an interesting recipe for making a cake in a coffee can, and that was my starting point. I made a great yellow cake batter, creaming the butter and sugar, adding the eggs, folding in the flour and other dry ingredients, and then pouring it into the coffee can and baking. The result was very charred outside and raw inside. I could not get the cake out of the can. The recipe was written for a dense fruitcake, and I am sure I did not even read the recipe.

I cried a lot, and my siblings enjoyed laughing at the inedible results. My wise mother was sympathetic, hugged me, and told me how much she appreciated the effort I made to prepare something just for her. It was a first step in learning to let go, not get discouraged, and continue to do something I loved. I am so glad I did not give up.

I threw away my birthday-cake mishap, but many times a disaster can be recreated into something surprisingly wonderful. In comparison to my earlier disaster, I am happy to say I have created many new and delicious dishes, and you can, too.

This is a great exercise in self-care and kindness. It is OK to mess up and make mistakes. Please allow others in your household who cook to learn from making their own mistakes, too.

Solo Practice

Cooking as a solo venture can be a good way to reduce stress after a busy day.

If you are cooking for an impatient group, put out some healthy nibbles to satisfy their hunger and have some quiet time in the kitchen. Avoid those salty, sweet snacks that fill you up and dull your appetite and, rather, offer a mini part of the meal. When my children were younger, I would put out a plate of their favorite raw vegetables and a dressing to dip them in or a simple salad for them to eat while I prepared the rest of the meal. Try offering a small cup of warm soup or broth in the cooler months.

While you are cooking, indulge in your own relaxation practice. Focus on breathing, listen to calming music, or enjoy the peacefulness that silence can bring.

Preparing a meal can be a spiritual practice. When you wash, cut, and cook the ingredients, concentrate on one task at a time. Be present while performing each step, and observe the beautiful patterns and colors of real foods. Breathe in the subtle aromas of cooking. Give the ingredients the loving attention they deserve. Your energy is part of what is going into creating the food you will be eating. Turn off the voice inside of you that is telling you to hurry up because you do not have enough time.

NOURISHMENT PRACTICE

Make a list of things in your life you can let go of so you can enjoy the process of cooking. Pick one or two meals each week that you plan to prepare with relaxed intention; note what you discover.

Positive Thoughts
Cooking is a relaxing practice that I embrace and enjoy.

FAMILY AND COMMUNITY COOKING

Cooking with family members or a larger community can give you the opportunity to see the bigger picture and embrace the needs of others.

Each person, regardless of age, can bring something valuable to the table when cooking a meal. Most children love to put their hands in water and can easily wash vegetables in the sink with a scrub brush. Letting children prepare an age-appropriate dish can build confidence and can often get them to try new foods. Be sure to include those individuals who are shy and who may not step forward when things are too chaotic.

During my awkward teenage years, I looked forward to the holidays my family spent with my aunt and uncle. My aunt always allowed me to help her in the kitchen, arrange the simple appetizer on plates, pick out special serving dishes for the crackers, and set the table with her special china and silver. I felt loved, accepted, and special. I was lucky to have this, and I encourage you to share these simple gestures with those around you. There is a place for everyone in the kitchen.

A meal that is nourishing and prepared by a group of people requires compromise, acceptance, and love. Please plan to prepare dishes that are nourishing for you. However, more importantly, think about whom you will be sharing the dishes with, and make them feel welcome.

NOURISHMENT PRACTICE

The next time you are joining family, friends to share a meal or any time you sit down to eat focus on this practice. Let go of the idea of perfection and sit down with the intent to relax and enjoy the meal. Take a few minutes to choose the foods that will nourish you best and eat them slowly. Focus on those with whom you are sharing the meal and appreciate your time together.

Positive Thoughts
I love and accept all those with whom I share a meal with, regardless of their choices.

CHAPTER 6

WHEN TO STAY OUT OF THE KITCHEN

As MUCH AS I enjoy the process and end result of creating a delicious meal, there are times when it is in your best interest to bless your kitchen space and close the door.

If you are feeling angry, upset, or emotionally unbalanced, find a way to recognize and accept what is happening. If you are angry when you are cooking, you will be eating your anger and so will those around you. If you can, take some time to step out of the situation and ask for help. If possible, get out of the kitchen, go for a walk, open a window and breathe in some fresh air, or call a friend.

A simple meal is a better choice than a complicated one when you are feeling upset, overwhelmed, anxious, or obligated. Learn to recognize that these feelings point to deeper issues that you need to look at. Resist the impulse to stuff the feelings away or dismiss them, which will not make them go away. Maybe this is the night to order takeout. If these are feelings that you are experiencing on a regular basis, find support or professional help.

One of my female clients was a stay-at-home mom with three small children. Her partner traveled a lot and was away from home one week per month. She struggled with all of the day-to-day tasks involved in taking care of herself and her children. By dinnertime, she was frazzled. She had to feed herself and her children, and she needed to take a new approach. Meals prepared when her husband was away became simple, family-favorite dishes: cheese-and-bean quesadillas that she made in advance and put in the freezer, omelets, soup, and takeout on the last night. She also had picnics at the park with her friend and her children. They all enjoyed this routine together. The children were more relaxed at meals, and having a plan greatly reduced their mom's stress, too.

It's OK to Skip a Meal Now and Then

The quality of food we eat on a daily basis and having a regular rhythm with regard to meals is important in maintaining overall health. I have seen different kinds of eating schedules work for different clients at different times in their lives. Creating a nutritionally well-balanced plan that suits your needs and your lifestyle is a good starting place for everyone.

More importantly, practice slowing down in order to start listening to the signs your body gives you when it needs food. Babies are naturally attuned to the need for nourishment and let us know they are hungry when they become fussy and cry. As we grow and learn about the world around us, we sometimes eat for reasons other than hunger, and our bodies' signals become distorted.

When is the last time you experienced physical signs of hunger? These signs are different in everyone, but a grumbling stomach, a dip in energy level, light-headedness, irritability, and an inability to focus can indicate that your body needs nutrition.

Have you ever felt ravenously hungry and noticed that that feeling disappeared after drinking a few glasses of water? This is a common symptom of dehydration, which is sometimes confused with hunger.

Do not skip meals on a regular basis as a weight-loss tool, since this can negatively affect blood-sugar levels, metabolism, and brain function.

For most people, intermittent fasting or occasionally skipping a meal, which is practiced in many spiritual traditions, can be cleansing for body and mind. Consider eating your last meal of the day no later than 7:00 p.m. or between two and three hours before sleep. When you are ready to go to sleep, your body can rest and repair itself instead of spending its energy trying to digest the meal you just ate.

If you have overindulged in foods that do not support your best health, have digestive issues, are dealing with a stressful situation, or are sick, reducing food intake can give your body a rest while it heals. Please make sure to keep properly hydrated at these times. A simplified eating plan of easy to digest broths, fresh made vegetable juices and other nutrient dense whole foods can be cleansing and healing.

Nourishment Practice

Slow down and listen to the signals your body is giving you before eating. Ask yourself: am I feeling hungry? Notice how your body responds. Try sipping a glass of water and see if anything changes. If you still feel hungry, choose the best food you can and eat it slowly. Adopt a slower pace of eating your meals. Notice how long it takes you to eat your next meal. Commit to slowing down, adding 5-10 minutes of time to eating your meals during this next week. Make note of your observations.

Positive Thoughts
I listen deeply, respect my body's individual needs, and feed it with self-care and love.

CHAPTER 7

APPRECIATE: MAKE IT BEAUTIFUL, MAKE IT FUN

MY FAVORITE PART of the meal is right before sitting down to eat. Choose a place that relaxes you, make it special, and be thankful for what you are about to take in. If you are dining with your family or friends, in a large group, or just by yourself, don't skip these few extra steps—it's like the icing on the cake, that little extra sparkle that just makes all of your efforts that much more worthwhile.

Where we choose to eat our meals is just as important as the food on our plates. Cooks working in professional kitchens are notorious for having bad eating habits, skipping meals, or just nibbling on something at their workstations.

I recall one of my early experiences in a professional kitchen. I was working in a large conference-center kitchen. We had a scheduled lunch break each day after serving our guests. One of the cooks suggested we eat outside, and this soon became a regular practice. We ate sitting on a picnic blanket under the nearest tree. Getting out of my working environment allowed me to relax, to feel the breeze on my face, and to clear my mind so I could slow down and enjoy my meal.

How can you expect to feel energized if you eat while talking on the phone, standing up, getting ready to move on to the next task on your list, sitting at your desk, or driving your car? You do have time to step away from your desk, to turn off your phone, and to focus only on the activity of eating your meal, even if it is just for ten minutes.

Resist the urge to sit in front of the television or computer screen while eating. This habit disconnects you from fully engaging with the food on your plate and from those around you. It is hard to carry on a conversation. Sometimes when there is not enough self-care in our daily lives, disconnecting becomes a way to restore energy. Can you find another way to respect your needs and those of the people around you?

When you are at home, expand the possibilities of where you eat beyond the kitchen and dining room. Appreciate the beauty of the natural world by eating outdoors when the weather permits. Sit out on your porch steps and enjoy the cool night air, or eat under the glow of moonlight. Consider sharing a meal eaten in silence, slowing down, appreciating the good things in your life, and letting go of stressors.

Let in the Light and Bring Nature Inside

On dark, dreary days and during cold winter months, surround yourself with the soft flicker of candlelight. If you have a fireplace or wood stove in your home, partake in a cozy meal warmed by the light of the flames and notice how peaceful it can be.

Children and adults alike enjoy the element of spontaneity. Pull out a picnic blanket on a cold winter night, and have dinner on the living-room floor or in a homemade blanket tent lit with flashlights.

When my children were small, some of the prettiest tables we set were decorated with rocks, sticks, bird feathers, crystals, acorns, and bouquets of wild flowers that they gathered on our walks.

Each time we sit down to a meal, either by ourselves or in the company of others, we are acknowledging our aliveness in the world. Now is the time to be self-indulgent and celebrate. Be present, show appreciation, give thanks, and savor the gifts the earth provides; take it all in and take your time.

NOURISHMENT PRACTICE

How can you add another level of nourishment to your meal? Write down two to three ideas that you would like to try this week.

Positive Thoughts
I am grateful for each meal I partake in and know it provides me with all that I need.

CHAPTER 8

CHOOSING HEALTHY FOODS

WHAT YOU DON'T eat is just as important as what you do!

When we talk about purchasing and eating healthy foods, what exactly does that mean? Annemarie Colbin, founder of the Natural Gourmet Institute in New York, developed seven criteria for food selection. My list is based on many of her recommendations. Use these guidelines when planning menus and choosing ingredients.

REAL FOODS FIRST

Choose foods with one ingredient as they are found in nature, with all edible parts intact.

INDIVIDUAL NEEDS

Select foods and ingredients that support a person's current health condition, age, developmental stage, and lifestyle.

SUSTAINABILITY

Pick diverse foods that support healthy environmental practices: water conservation, energy efficiency, humane practice in how animals are raised and workers are treated, sustainability practices and safeguards for workers' health.

FRESH FOODS

Embrace foods that are vital and alive; these are best grown organically, with no GMOs or irradiation, and locally in healthy soil.

TRADITIONALLY PRESERVED AND CULTURED FOODS

Choose dried, pickled, fermented, and cultured foods preserved using nontoxic methods of preservation, without chemicals and colorings.

EAT ACCORDING TO THE SEASON

Plan menus, shop, and eat foods that are in season where you live as much as possible.

BALANCED NUTRIENTS AND PORTIONS

Plan meals around food balanced with the right quantities of essential nutrients for your stage in life and health status. Serve portion sizes that are appropriate for the individual.

PLEASURE AND NOURISHMENT

The food we eat and the experience of eating need to satisfy our senses. We should derive pleasure as well as nourishment from what we consume. Food is a sacred gift meant to be enjoyed and shared.

CHAPTER 9

SEASONAL RECIPES:
A FEW OF MY FAVORITE THINGS

THIS CHAPTER INCLUDES some of my favorite seasonal recipes. All are plant based, gluten, soy, and dairy-free, and I have suggested variations and pairings to make it easy to plan a meal. Get comfortable preparing the recipes. Have fun experimenting, using leftovers, including a beautiful seasonal vegetable you brought home from the farmers market, or letting diners add their favorite condiments. It is easy to include nourishing, high-quality organic dairy products, clean sources of animal protein, and substitute ingredients.

You can explore your neighborhood as well as expand your circle of options by changing your shopping habits. Invite a few friends on an outing to shop for food and to seek out local treasures, such as farms, local producers, and organic markets. Join a food co-op, invest in a seasonal community-supported agriculture group, or volunteer your time to a community garden. Engage in conversation about the state of our food supply and about how the foods we eat are grown. Become educated and empowered to make better choices for you and your family.

Pick a recipe you like, and use the coordinating **Pairing Guide** that accompanies each recipe for ideas you can use to build a meal. Have fun, try something new, experiment with your own combinations, and do not worry if the final product does not turn out as you planned. Congratulations on spending quality time investing in your health, and happy cooking!

BREAKFAST: SWEET AND SAVORY

My Favorite Green Scramble

Hazelnut-Cranberry Scones

Broth Bowls

Breakfast Oats: Warm Weather and Cold Weather

Root Vegetable Pancakes

Parfaits

My Favorite Green Scramble

Kale, Swiss chard, dandelion greens, bok choy, collard greens, arugula, spinach, wild-foraged greens, and watercress all fall into the category of dark, leafy greens.

I have not always been a lover of these types of greens. However, when I learned about their benefits, I started looking for ways to incorporate them into all of my meals. Dark, leafy greens are anti-inflammatory and support the function of the immune system. They are nutrient-dense whole foods that are rich in vitamins A, C, and D. Dark, leafy greens aid in digestion and in elimination. Most of these types of greens are good sources of chlorophyll, calcium, and iron. Dark, leafy greens also taste great.

This is one of my favorite easy breakfasts, especially when I have a long, busy day ahead. Leftover sautéed greens are great to have on hand. However, if you don't have these, fresh greens cook quickly.

Servings: 1

Ingredients:
1 to 2 cups chopped greens, of your choice
1-teaspoon coconut oil or grass-fed butter
¼ cup onion, leeks or shallots, sliced
1 egg, organic or from pasture-raised chicken
Salt and pepper to taste

Method:
Warm a small sauté pan over medium heat.
Add a teaspoon of coconut oil or grass-fed butter.
Add sliced onion, leeks, or shallots, and sauté for a few minutes until soft and translucent.
Add a handful or two of washed, chopped greens of your choice. Alternatively, use those leftover sautéed greens in your refrigerator.

Sauté for several minutes until wilted and softened. Season with natural salt and pepper.

Scramble the egg and pour over sautéed greens, stirring to combine. The egg mixture should be just enough to hold everything together.

Cover the pan, turn heat to low, and cook for a few minutes until set. Gently lift your green scramble onto a plate.

Add a topping, if desired, and enjoy! (A dash or two of hot sauce or a few tablespoons of salsa are my favorite toppings.)

You can replace eggs with ground grass fed beef, bison or organic tofu. Crumble tofu and sauté with onions before adding greens.

PAIRING GUIDE:
Goat cheese
Whole-grain, gluten-free, or Paleo-style wrap
Oven-roasted rosemary garlic tomato
Pumpkin-seed pesto
Spinach "ricotta"

NOTES:

HAZELNUT-CRANBERRY SCONES

Finely ground, sweet-tasting hazelnuts make a good substitute for flour and are an excellent source of calcium.

Servings: 8

INGREDIENTS:

2 cups finely ground hazelnuts
¾ cup organic rolled oats
½ cup organic dried cranberries, fruit-juice sweetened
½-teaspoon natural salt
1-teaspoon baking powder
2 to 3 tablespoons maple syrup, raw honey, or Xylitol
2 organic eggs, large
1-teaspoon vanilla extract

METHOD:

Preheat oven to 350 degrees.

Combine ground hazelnuts, oats, cranberries, salt, and baking powder in a bowl, and stir to combine.

In a small bowl, mix together maple syrup, eggs, and vanilla.

Pour egg mixture into dry ingredients, and stir to combine until mixture comes together.

Pat dough into a ball, flatten with hands into a disc shape, and roll into a 7-inch to 8-inch circle.

Place dough on a baking pan lined with parchment paper.

With a sharp knife, mark dough into portions by cutting three-quarters of the way through into eight even sections.

Sprinkle top of scones with cinnamon, if desired.

Bake scones for fifteen to twenty minutes until golden brown on bottom and lightly toasted on top.

Remove scones from oven, and cool slightly before serving.

CHEF NOTES AND VARIATIONS:

Ground hazelnut flour is available in many markets, or you can grind your own in a high-powered blender.

Substitute hazelnut flour with almond flour.

Store cooled scones in sealed container.

Scones are delicious as is or toasted and topped with fruit jam, coconut butter, or your favorite topping.

PAIRING GUIDE:

Fruit jam or Fruit Butter

Coconut butter (warmed up in toaster)

Coconut whipped cream and fresh berries (makes a shortcake dessert)

Grass-fed butter

COCONUT WHIPPED CREAM:

Chill a 14-ounce can of full-fat organic coconut milk in the refrigerator overnight.

Drain liquid from can (reserve for another use).

Place solid coconut cream in a chilled mixing bowl.

Whisk coconut cream with metal whisk until fluffy. Add 1 teaspoon of vanilla extract and 1 tablespoon of sweetener of your choice.

NOTES:

BROTH BOWLS

Vegetable broth, mushroom broth, miso broth, Asian-style broth, and bone broth are all very popular—and for good reason. Homemade broths that are made with high-quality ingredients are dense with nutrients, hydrating, easy to digest, and delicious. Broth is also a convenient meal and perfect for a quick breakfast as part of a healing diet or weight-loss program. For those with a small appetite and low energy, sipping on a healing broth is an easy way to get in nutrition.

With the addition of flavoring, vegetables, and noodles or grains, broth bowls are easy to put together and make a great cold-weather breakfast that is warm, cozy, and satisfying.

START WITH THE BROTH:
Use garlic-onion broth or your favorite vegetable or bone broth. Add your choice of additional flavorings, but do not overdo it.

INGREDIENTS TO CHOOSE:
2 to 3 slices fresh, peeled ginger
1 to 2 cloves garlic, crushed or sliced
Dash or more of toasted sesame oil
Sliced shitake mushrooms or dried porcini mushrooms
Sea vegetables (Wakame or Dulse)
Miso (chickpea miso is a good, gluten-free option)
Dash of chili oil, crushed red pepper flakes, or jalapeño
Minced fresh herbs: cilantro, chives, basil, lemongrass, or parsley
Minced scallions

EXTRA GOODIES:
Leftover cooked vegetables cut into small pieces
Shredded carrots, daikon radish, or small pieces of broccoli
Bean sprouts
Leftover chicken or beef, cut into small pieces

Tofu or tempeh, cut into small pieces
Leftover sautéed greens
Leftover grains, such as quinoa or brown rice
Udon, buckwheat, or rice noodles
More mushrooms
Crack an egg into the simmering broth and let it cook for two to three minutes or until done.

NOTES:

Breakfast Oats: Warm Weather and Cold Weather

Soaking grains is a traditional preparation technique. If you include grains in your diet, soaking them is a simple additional step that will help to break down the antinutrients and make them easier to digest and assimilate.

WARM-WEATHER BREAKFAST OATS

Raw oats soaked overnight with the addition of flavorings produces a chewy, textured easy-to-eat cereal. Add your favorite berries, nuts, fruits, and other toppings. Make several varieties, one for each day of the week.

INGREDIENTS:

⅓ Cup rolled oats (not quick-cooking oats)
⅓ Cup water, almond milk, coconut milk, or other nondairy variety
½-teaspoon vanilla extract
½-teaspoon lemon juice, fresh
Pinch of natural salt

METHOD:

Place oats in glass jar. Add liquid, vanilla, lemon juice, and salt, and stir to combine.
Place lid on jar and refrigerate overnight; oats are ready to eat in the morning!
Stir in your favorite nuts, seeds, berries, sweetener, fresh fruit, or other spices before eating, or layer them in before soaking.

COLD-WEATHER BREAKFAST OATS

Steel-cut oats are the perfect make-ahead breakfast; they are easy to reheat and stay creamy for several days.

INGREDIENTS:

1 cup steel-cut oats, rinsed
1-tablespoon coconut oil

3 cups water
½-teaspoon natural salt
1 teaspoon cinnamon, ground
1-teaspoon vanilla extract
1-tablespoon lemon juice, fresh
1 to 1½ cups almond, coconut, or your favorite milk

Method:

Heat coconut oil over medium heat in saucepan. Toast oats in oil for three to five minutes until fragrant, dry, and lightly golden.

Add water, salt, cinnamon, and vanilla to oats. Bring to a boil, stir, and turn off heat. Stir in lemon juice, and cover with lid.

Refrigerate oats overnight.

When ready to serve, bring mixture to a boil. Add almond milk, stir, and turn down to a simmer. Cook for several minutes until heated through. Top oats with fresh fruit, nuts, seeds, coconut flakes, favorite sweetener, dairy-free yogurt, or other toppings.

Notes:

ROOT VEGETABLE PANCAKES

Potato pancakes or Rösti potatoes are crispy, pan-fried pancakes made with a starchy potato, sometimes with a little egg added, and seasoned with salt and pepper. I learned how to perfect these when I was apprenticing in a German restaurant. In this version, I use sweet potato, ground golden flaxseed, and nutritious root vegetables.

Servings: 4 to 8 pancakes, depending on size

INGREDIENTS:

1½ pounds sweet potato, russet potato, or a combination, peeled and grated
½-pound root vegetables: carrots, beets, parsnips, kohlrabi, or whatever kind you like, peeled and grated
¼ cup onion, grated
1 clove garlic, minced
2 tablespoons golden flaxseed, ground
6 tablespoons water
1-teaspoon natural salt
2 teaspoons chives or thyme leaves, minced
Coconut oil or coconut-oil spray for frying

METHOD:

Grate sweet potato and root vegetables, and place in mixing bowl.
Mix golden flaxseed in a small bowl with water to combine, and let rest for ten minutes.
Add onion, garlic, salt, and herbs to grated vegetables and mix.
Add flaxseed/water mixture to vegetables, and gently combine until thoroughly mixed.
Heat a well-seasoned sauté pan over medium heat. Add 1 to 2 teaspoons coconut oil and lightly coat the bottom of the pan. Add small amount of potato-pancake mixture to pan, depending on size of pancakes you want. Press pancake down lightly with back of spatula.

Cook pancakes for six- eight minutes on each side or until a nice golden crust has formed. Turn pancake over and cook until browned and crispy.

Cook remaining pancake mixture. Serve pancakes hot, as is, or with your choice of toppings.

CHEF NOTES AND VARIATIONS:

Pancakes can be made in advance and frozen or refrigerated.

Depending on vegetable combination, you may need to add a few tablespoons of gluten-free flour so that the ingredients stick together.

Replace golden flaxseed and water mixture with two eggs.

PAIRING GUIDE:

Leftover sautéed greens

Applesauce or sautéed apples

Fried egg and hot sauce

Horseradish coconut cream

Sautéed leeks

Cheddar cheese and chili sauce

Maple syrup and toasted pecans

HORSERADISH COCONUT CREAM:

Chill a 14-ounce can of full-fat organic coconut milk in the refrigerator overnight.

Drain liquid from can (reserve for another use).

Place solid coconut cream in a chilled mixing bowl.

Whisk coconut cream with metal whisk until fluffy. Add 1 to 2 teaspoons of prepared horseradish, a squeeze of fresh lemon juice, a pinch of salt, and one tablespoon of fresh, minced chives or scallions.

NOTES:

PARFAITS

Parfaits, dating back to the late eighteen hundreds, originated in France. These cold desserts are traditionally made with layers of ice cream, fruit/berries, whipped cream, and sometimes a splash of liqueur. Parfaits are served in tall glasses to display the layers of delicious and colorful ingredients inside. The word "parfait" translates in French to "perfect."

I love the idea of layering ingredients in a fancy glass and placing it on a pretty dish on top of a paper doily. This dessert is something that calls out to be eaten slowly, one layer at a time, or taking a bit of each layer in one bite and savoring different flavor combinations.

Parfaits are simple to make and fun to eat. You can make them with healthy ingredients and eat them for breakfast, dessert, or a snack. Involve the kids or your guests in creating their own combinations. These also make a great to-go meal, layered in a glass jar, though you will be missing the fancy-glass experience.

LET'S TALK LAYERS

SOMETHING CREAMY:
(Besides ice cream)
Yogurt: choose organic dairy or yogurt made with almond or coconut milk
Coconut milk kefir
Whipped coconut cream or organic whipped cream flavored with vanilla extract
Frozen bananas made into creamy base in a food processor or a high-speed blender
Vanilla cashew cream

FRUITY DELICIOUSNESS:
(Let the season be your guide.)
Seasonal berries or frozen berries: strawberries, blueberries, raspberries or wild berries

Fresh fruits sliced or cut into pieces: peaches, apples, pears, banana, plums, kiwi, figs, or grapes

Dried fruits cut into small pieces: figs, raisins, cranberries, goji berries, dried mango, or golden berries

Fruit jam without added sweeteners

A LITTLE CRUNCH:

Chopped toasted nuts: almonds, hazelnuts, pecans, sunflower seeds, coconut flakes, or walnuts

Granola: homemade or store bought

Cookies: broken up into small pieces

Grain-free granola made with seeds, nuts, and coconut flakes

Dare I say—chocolate! Chocolate chips, shaved chocolate, cacao nibs, or cocoa powder

CHEF NOTES AND VARIATIONS:

Make it a do-it-yourself dessert for a fun event or a kids' tea party.

NOTES:

Refrigerator Magic:
Dressings and Condiments

Peachy Tomato-Basil Dressing

Pumpkin-Seed Pesto

Sesame-Ginger Carrot Dressing

Almond-Sunflower-Seed Spread with Roasted Garlic

Spicy Pickled Red Onions

Oven-Roasted Rosemary with Garlic Tomato

Italian-Herb Vinaigrette

PEACHY TOMATO-BASIL DRESSING

Make this dressing when tomatoes and peaches are in season, juicy, and ripe.

Servings: 1½ cups

INGREDIENTS:

1 cup or 1 large tomato, very ripe, diced, with juices included
½ cup peach, very ripe, peeled and diced, with juices included
½-cup basil leaves, washed and loosely packed
1 clove garlic, peeled
1 to 2 tablespoons Umeboshi vinegar or cider vinegar
¼ cup extra-virgin olive oil
Salt and pepper to season

METHOD:

Place tomato, peaches, basil, garlic, vinegar, and olive oil in a blender with lid.
Blend mixture for one minute, or until it is well combined and smooth.
Taste dressing and season as needed.

CHEF NOTES AND VARIATIONS:

Substitute basil with other fresh herbs, such as tarragon, parsley, or thyme, adjusting amounts as needed.

Pairing Guide:
Grilled zucchini or eggplant
Black beans and tortilla or other grain-free chips
Poached or grilled fish or chicken
Fresh mozzarella or Burrata cheese and arugula
Roasted peppers
Grilled fennel
Jalapeño or other hot peppers and your favorite burger or vegetarian bean burger

Notes:

PUMPKIN-SEED PESTO
A yummy nut-free pesto

Servings: 2 cups

INGREDIENTS:
1 cup parsley leaves, washed
1-cup spinach leaves, washed and spun dry
1-cup basil leaves, washed and spun dry
¾ cup pumpkin seeds, shelled and lightly toasted
1 to 2 cloves garlic, peeled
1/3 cup olive oil
1 to 2 tablespoons fresh lemon juice, strained
¼-cup nutritional yeast
Natural salt and fresh ground pepper to taste

METHOD:
Place toasted pumpkin seeds and garlic in bowl of food processor fitted
with an S-shaped blade. Process until chunky.
Add parsley, spinach, and basil. Pulse until greens are in small pieces.
Add olive oil, lemon juice, nutritional yeast, and process until smooth.
Scrape down bowl in between processing to ensure even mixing.
Season with salt and pepper to taste.

CHEF NOTES AND VARIATIONS:
Thin pesto with a little water or broth to make a sauce.
Substitute basil and spinach with other fresh herb and greens variations,
such as cilantro, arugula, oregano, parsley, and chives.

PAIRING GUIDE:
Broccoli Almond fritters
Pan-seared salmon
Roasted sweet-potato wedges
Rice noodles and roasted vegetables

NOTES:

SESAME-GINGER CARROT DRESSING

Sesame seeds are a good source of protein, vitamin E, and calcium. Rinse sesame seeds and toast them for a few minutes in a pan on top of the stove for the best flavor.

Servings: 1¼ cups

INGREDIENTS:

4 tablespoons brown-rice vinegar
2 tablespoons coconut amino or tamari
2 teaspoons ginger, grated
2 teaspoons toasted sesame oil
1 clove garlic, minced
⅔ cup olive oil
1 tablespoon scallions, minced
½ cup carrot, finely grated
1-tablespoon sesame seeds, toasted
Dash of hot sauce for a pop of spicy flavor

METHOD:

Blend vinegar, coconut amino, ginger, toasted sesame oil, garlic, and olive oil in blender for one to two minutes to combine.

Add scallions, carrot, and toasted sesame seeds. Pulse for a few seconds to combine.

Taste and adjust seasonings as necessary. Add hot sauce.

CHEF NOTES AND VARIATIONS:

Use leftover carrot pulp from juicing instead of grated carrot.
Dressing will keep in the refrigerator for several weeks.

PAIRING GUIDE:
Grilled fish
Sautéed snap peas or green beans
Sautéed greens
Steamed broccoli and grilled chicken
Pan-seared tempeh or tofu
Sliced beef and mixed salad greens
Sea vegetable and radish

NOTES:

ALMOND-SUNFLOWER-SEED SPREAD WITH ROASTED GARLIC

This rich and satisfying spread is perfect as a cracker or flatbread topper and a good protein-rich addition to any meal.

Servings: 6 to 8

INGREDIENTS:

1-cup raw almonds, soaked overnight in water, drained, with skins removed

½ cup raw sunflower seeds, soaked overnight and drained

2 tablespoons nutritional yeast

½-teaspoon natural salt

1 bulb garlic, roasted and peeled

1 to 2 tablespoons fresh lemon juice

¾ cup water

1 carrot, peeled, medium diced

¼ cup red onion, minced

¼ cup Italian parsley leaves

METHOD:

Place soaked, drained, and peeled almonds in bowl of food processor fitted with S blade. Add soaked and drained sunflower seeds.

Process nuts until ground.

Add nutritional yeast, salt, garlic, and lemon and process. Slowly add water, and continue to process until smooth and creamy. Scrape down nut mixture during blending to ensure an even consistency.

Add carrots, red onion, and parsley. Pulse for thirty to sixty seconds until combined.

Taste and add extra seasoning if necessary.

CHEF NOTES AND VARIATIONS:

To vary flavors, add other fresh herbs, such as cilantro, chives, thyme, or basil.

PAIRING GUIDE:

Raw vegetables

Nori sheets and sprouts and shredded carrots

Baked sweet potato

Crackers or whole-grain/gluten-free bread

Pear and apple slices and fresh figs

Grain free wrap with avocado, tomato and lettuce

NOTES:

Spicy Pickled Red Onions

Quick pickled onions are easy to make. Pickling softens and takes away the sharp raw onion flavor. Use raw, unfiltered apple cider vinegar, which is high in mineral content.

Servings: 1-pint jar

Ingredients:

1 large red or sweet onion, peeled and thinly sliced
1 jalapeño pepper, thinly sliced (add as many seeds as you want, depending on how spicy you like it)
2 cloves garlic, peeled and smashed
3 sprigs thyme
1 cup raw, unfiltered, unpasteurized organic apple-cider vinegar
1½ teaspoons natural salt
1 to 2 tablespoons maple syrup or a few drops of liquid Stevia

Method:

Layer onion, jalapeño, garlic, and thyme into clean one-pint glass jar, pushing down onion to pack firmly.
Mix together apple cider vinegar, salt, and sweetener.
Pour liquid over onions until it covers them, leaving one inch of space at top of jar.
Seal jar with lid.
Let onion soften and pickle for several hours or until it is at desired consistency.
Refrigerate onion. It will continue to soften and is best eaten within 1 to 2 weeks.

Chef Notes and Variations:

Substitute jalapeño peppers with a dash of crushed red pepper or omit completely.

Pairing Guide:
Broccoli Almond fritters
Organic beef or turkey burger and blue cheese or sharp cheddar cheese
Shredded green cabbage and grated carrots
Grilled chicken and grilled pineapple
Fish and taco shells and shredded lettuce
Refried beans
Polenta, chilies, and cheese
Roasted potato

Notes:

OVEN-ROASTED ROSEMARY WITH GARLIC CHERRY TOMATOES

Delicious right out of the oven or at room temperature, these make a good addition to pasta, roasted vegetables, or pizza.

Servings: 2 cups

INGREDIENTS:

2 pints cherry tomatoes (yellow, orange, or red), washed and patted dry
6 cloves garlic, peeled and pressed
1 tablespoon rosemary, minced
2 tablespoons coconut oil, warmed so it is liquid
Salt and freshly ground pepper to taste

METHOD:

Preheat oven to 375 degrees.

Place tomatoes, garlic, rosemary, and coconut oil in bowl, and mix to combine.

Place cherry tomatoes in a single layer on a parchment-lined sheet pan.

Sprinkle the top of tomatoes with salt and a grind of fresh pepper.

Bake in oven for about thirty-five minutes, or until softened and roasted. (The tomatoes should not be totally collapsed and should maintain their shape.)

Pairing Guide:
Pizza crust and arugula
Roasted spaghetti squash
Salmon or chicken
Grilled polenta and pumpkin-seed pesto
Black beans, corn, and fresh cilantro
Sautéed kale or other greens
Grilled Portobello mushrooms
Cooked lentils
Roasted cauliflower and dairy or nondairy cheese
Grilled eggplant

Notes:

ITALIAN-HERB VINAIGRETTE

Grab a jar meant for recycling or one of your canning jars and shake up a basic vinaigrette-style dressing. I make this dressing most often, it's a versatile refrigerator staple.

Servings: 1-1/2 cups

INGREDIENTS:

½ cup olive oil, cold pressed, organic
¼ cup fresh lemon juice, fresh
¼ cup cider vinegar (raw, organic, and unfiltered)
2 teaspoon Dijon mustard or dry mustard
1 clove garlic, pressed
1 tablespoon capers, rinsed and chopped
2 tablespoons shallots or fresh chives, finely minced
2 teaspoons Italian herb seasoning, dry (basil, oregano, thyme)
2 tablespoons nutritional yeast
Salt and freshly ground pepper to taste

METHOD:

Place all of the ingredients in a jar, twist lid to secure, and shake vigorously to incorporate.
Taste dressing and adjust seasonings as necessary.

CHEF NOTES AND VARIATIONS:

If the vinegar you are using is very sharp, try adding a few tablespoons of apple juice to sweeten and balance the flavor.

Pairing Guide:

Salad greens and toasted walnuts or slivered almonds
Cooked lentils and roasted vegetables
Stir-fried vegetables
Roasted peppers and mushrooms
Heirloom tomato, Kalamata olives, and artichoke hearts
Grilled vegetables and shaved Pecorino Romano cheese
Cucumber, watermelon radish, and avocado

Notes:

Soups and Stews

Creamy Summer Squash and Basil Soup

Garlic Onion Broth with Greens

Sweet Potato, Black Bean, and Kale Stew

Curried Chickpea and Vegetable Stew

CREAMY SUMMER SQUASH AND BASIL SOUP

Tender, soft-skinned yellow summer squash is the star ingredient in this simple summer soup. Add fresh basil right before serving for a burst of flavor.

Servings: 6 to 8

INGREDIENTS:

1-tablespoon olive oil
1 cup onion, peeled and diced
5 stalks celery, diced
½ teaspoon dried thyme leaves
1¼ pounds summer squash, trimmed, washed, and diced
4 cups vegetable stock
¼ cup fresh basil leaves
Natural salt and fresh pepper to taste

METHOD:

Heat olive oil over low-to-medium heat in five- or six-quart saucepan.
Add onions and celery, and sauté for three to five minutes, until softened.
Add thyme leaves and summer squash, and sauté for two to three minutes.
Add vegetable stock to saucepan, and bring to a boil.
Turn heat down to a simmer, cover saucepan, and cook for fifteen to twenty-five minutes, until the squash is just tender. Do not overcook.
Puree soup in blender or with immersion-style blender until desired consistency is achieved.
Add fresh basil, and blend for a short time to combine.
Season with salt and pepper as needed.
Serve soup warm.

CHEF NOTES AND VARIATIONS:

Younger, delicate summer squash is best for this soup. If you are using more mature squash, remove seeds.

Pairing Guide:
Lentils and red peppers
Chèvre
Spinach "ricotta"
Soft polenta
Baked tomato
Escarole and cannellini beans

Notes:

GARLIC ONION BROTH WITH GREENS

Garlic is a wonderful antibacterial and antiviral ingredient. This is a good soup to have on hand when you are feeling a little run-down. Onions and leeks help to promote warmth and to purify the body of heavy metals and toxins.

Servings: 6 to 8

INGREDIENTS:

3 bulbs garlic, separated into cloves, peeled, and smashed
1-tablespoon olive oil
2 cups leeks, trimmed, washed, and chopped (green and white parts)
1 carrot, scrubbed and chopped
2 stalks celery, cleaned and chopped
5 sprigs parsley
4 sprigs thyme
1 piece Kombu, 2-inch
1-teaspoon natural salt
3 quarts water
2 bunches dark, leafy greens: escarole, kale, spicy greens, watercress, mustard greens, arugula, Swiss chard, or your favorite foraged greens
2 teaspoons lemon juice
(Optional: extra raw garlic for a fresh pop of garlicky goodness)

METHOD:

Place a large, heavy-bottomed stockpot over medium heat. Add oil, garlic, leeks, carrots, celery, and sauté until vegetables are softened.

Add water, parsley, thyme, Kombu, and salt. Bring stock to a boil, and immediately turn down to a simmer. Cook for thirty to forty-five minutes, or until vegetables are soft.

Strain stock through a fine-mesh strainer (or use a nut-milk bag). Press and squeeze out as much liquid as possible. You should have between two and two and a half quarts of stock.

Place strained stock back into stockpot, and bring to a simmer.

Wash greens, trim off inedible stems if necessary, and chop into small pieces.

Add greens to the soup, and simmer until greens are just tender (time will vary depending on the greens you choose).

Taste soup; add additional salt if necessary and a squeeze of fresh lemon juice.

Chef Notes and Variations:

Serve warm soup in bowl. Add one clove raw, pressed garlic to each bowl before serving, if desired, and a splash of extra-virgin olive oil.

Pairing Guide:

Mini meatballs

Poached egg

Garlic Onion Broth + Red lentils

Extra vegetables

Shrimp or leftover fish

Wild mushrooms and buckwheat or rice noodles

Notes:

Sweet Potato, Black Bean, and Kale Stew

A warming, cool-weather stew, sweetened with flavors of root vegetables. A touch of crushed red pepper adds a hint of spice.

Servings:6-8

Ingredients:

2 tablespoons olive oil
1 cup leeks or onions, minced
3 garlic cloves, minced
2 carrots, scrubbed and diced
2 pounds sweet potato or garnet yams, peeled and medium diced
1 to 2 tablespoons ground cumin
2 teaspoons dried oregano
1½ quarts vegetable stock
15-ounces canned tomato with juice, diced
2 bay leaves, dry
2 cups black beans, cooked
1 large bunch kale, cleaned, stems removed, and cut into thin strips
1 pinch or more crushed red pepper
Salt and pepper to taste

Method:

Heat oil in medium-sized stockpot over low-medium heat. Sauté onions, garlic, and carrots until softened.

Add sweet potato, cumin, oregano, vegetable stock, tomato, bay leaves, and bring to a boil. Turn heat down to a simmer, and cook for thirty minutes until vegetables are soft.

Add black beans, kale, and crushed red pepper to stew, stir to combine, and cover. Cook for fifteen to twenty minutes until kale is tender.

Taste stew and adjust seasoning as needed with salt and pepper.

Serve stew warm.

CHEF NOTES AND Variations:
Substitute black beans with kidney beans.
Substitute kale for other dark leafy greens

PAIRING GUIDE:
Ground, grass-fed bison, turkey, or beef
Coconut milk

NOTES:

CURRIED CHICKPEA AND VEGETABLE STEW

Sweet coconut-milk broth with spicy curry seasoning is a comforting and warming food for chilly days.

Servings: 8

INGREDIENTS:

2 tablespoons coconut oil
3 cloves garlic, peeled and minced
2 small onions or leeks, trimmed, rinsed, and minced
1 to 2 tablespoons curry powder
¾-pound butternut or acorn squash, peeled and medium diced
2 cans coconut milk, 14 ounces each
1-cup water or vegetable stock
1-teaspoon natural salt
1 zucchini, medium to large, medium diced
2 cups chickpeas, cooked
1½ cups peas, fresh or frozen
2 tablespoons fresh cilantro, minced
2 tablespoons fresh basil, minced

TOPPINGS:

½ cup toasted almonds or cashew nuts, chopped
2 scallions, minced
¼ cup coconut, toasted

METHOD:

Heat large saucepan over medium heat, and add coconut oil. Sauté onions and garlic for a few minutes until onions begin to soften.
Add curry powder and stir. Toast curry lightly, being careful not to burn it. Add diced butternut squash and sauté for a few minutes.

Add coconut milk, water, and salt to sautéed vegetables. Bring mixture to a boil, turn down to simmer, and cook for eight to ten minutes until squash is soft.

Add zucchini and chickpeas, and simmer until vegetables are just tender.

Add peas, cilantro, and basil. Taste and adjust seasoning as needed.

Serve garnishes in small bowls on the side so guests can help themselves.

Pairing Guide:

Steamed brown rice or quinoa

Shrimp

Eggplant

Buckwheat or udon noodles

Sweet potato or garnet yams

Tofu or tempeh

Notes:

Lovely, Leaf Greens:

Simple Sautéed Greens

Wilted Spinach and Spicy Green Salad

Coconut Creamed Spinach

Strawberry Salad Bowl

Simple Sautéed Greens

Dark, leafy greens are an essential part of my diet. There are many ways to prepare greens depending on what you are working with, but this is still my go-to preparation method. Make a big batch. Leftovers reheat easily and can be incorporated into other dishes.

Servings: 2 to 4

Ingredients:

2 large bunches Swiss chard, kale, mustard greens, broccoli rabe, escarole, dandelion greens, spinach, collard greens, wild-foraged greens, or any of your favorites
2 cloves or more garlic, peeled and minced
1-tablespoon coconut oil or unrefined sesame oil
Pinch natural salt

Method:

Wash greens thoroughly in several changes of water to remove all dirt.
Cut greens into bite-sized pieces. (Remove stems from kale and collard greens—they are tough.)
Drain greens in colander, and lightly shake off excess water.
Heat large sauté pan over medium heat. Add oil and garlic, and sauté for several minutes until softened, being careful not to burn garlic.
Add greens, a little at a time, using tongs to toss. Combine with garlic and oil until all greens have been added.
Turn heat down to simmer. There should still be moisture on greens. If not, add a few tablespoons of water, cover pan, and cook for two to six minutes until desired consistency is reached. Cooking times will vary depending on what greens you are using.

Chef Notes and Variations:

Season with Gomasio Salt (ground sesame seeds, sea salt, and sea vegetable combination).

Add minced ginger or ginger juice and a dash of toasted sesame oil.
Add chopped Kalamata olives.
Add sliced, diced, or chopped onions in with garlic while sautéing.
Toss in any leftover cooked vegetables.
Add garlic paste (mashed garlic cloves mixed with 1-tablespoon olive oil and 1 tablespoon fresh lemon juice) at the end of cooking.
Add toasted sunflower seeds, hemp seeds, walnuts, or other favorites.
Add a splash of balsamic vinegar, lemon juice, cider vinegar, or Umeboshi vinegar for a tangy finish.
Add minced roasted peppers.
Add fresh or rehydrated tomato.
The possibilities are endless. Have fun!

PAIRING GUIDE:
Roasted mushrooms

Steamed fish

Pasta and oven-roasted tomato

Ground, grass-fed bison and gluten-free or other whole-grain wrap

Baked potato or baked yams and grass-fed butter or cheese

Pasta or rice noodles, toasted sesame oil, and coconut aminos

Chicken breast and roasted peppers

NOTES:

WILTED SPINACH AND SPICY GREEN SALAD

Wilted salads are a beautiful balance between crispy summer salad greens and sautéed heartier greens. This salad is a good first course for entertaining.

Servings: 6 (as a side dish)

INGREDIENTS:
1 pound baby spinach and spicy greens
4 tablespoons olive oil
1 small red onion, minced
1 clove garlic, crushed
1 teaspoon Dijon-style mustard
1 tablespoon maple syrup or raw honey
4 tablespoons raw apple-cider vinegar or fresh lemon juice
½ cup apple chips, dried, no sugar added, and cut into small pieces
¼ cup hemp seeds

METHOD:
Wash spinach and greens, dry, and cut into bite-sized pieces. Place cleaned greens in a bowl, and set aside.

Heat a small sauté pan over low-medium heat, and add olive oil, onion, and a pinch of salt. Sauté until onions are softened.

In a small bowl, combine crushed garlic, Dijon, maple syrup, and vinegar. Stir to combine.

Add vinegar mixture to sauté pan. Stir to combine.

Add apple chips and cook for several minutes until they soften and liquid reduces slightly and gets syrupy.

Remove pan from stove, and pour hot dressing over greens. Toss greens with dressing to combine; the greens will wilt. Taste and season with salt and pepper as needed.

Serve immediately on individual plates. Garnish with hemp seeds.

Chef Notes and Variations:
Substitute hemp seeds with chopped toasted walnuts or pumpkin seeds.

Pairing Guide:
Goat-cheese feta
Tempeh crouton or organic bacon
Roasted vegetables (winter squash, potato, carrots)
Roasted chickpeas
Pan-seared scallops or fish
Steamed quinoa

Notes:

COCONUT CREAMED SPINACH

Creamed spinach was a comfort food for me growing up, served occasionally with Sunday dinner. Here is a lighter version incorporating healthy fats from canned coconut cream.

Servings: 4

INGREDIENTS:

1 pound or 2 large bunches of spinach, cleaned and chopped into small pieces, and placed in colander
2 teaspoons coconut oil
½ cup onion, minced
3 cloves garlic, minced
5.4-ounce can coconut cream
½ teaspoon natural salt
¼ teaspoon nutmeg, ground
¼ cup water
2 teaspoons arrowroot powder

METHOD:

Heat medium-sized saucepan or a sauté pan that has a lid over medium heat, and add coconut oil.

Sauté onion and garlic for two to three until softened and lightly golden.

Add chopped spinach to sauté pan, and stir to combine.

Pour coconut cream over spinach. Add salt and nutmeg.

Cover pan with lid, and turn heat down to low. Cook for five to six minutes until spinach is wilted and tender.

In a small bowl, combine water and arrowroot powder, and stir to combine.

Pour arrowroot mixture into spinach, and stir to combine. Cook for two minutes or until liquid is thickened.

Serve spinach as is or use an immersion blender to puree it.

Pairing Guide:

Poached egg

Mashed potato or mashed cauliflower

Grilled Portobello mushrooms

Grilled bison steak

Pan-seared salmon and oven-roasted tomato

Crepes

Zucchini noodles made with spiralizer

Notes:

STRAWBERRY SALAD BOWL

Strawberries and arugula show up at our local farms at the same time. I enjoy this simple and refreshing salad. Raspberries, blueberries, and other wild berries are a good substitute.

Servings: 4 to 6

INGREDIENTS:

6 ounces arugula
1½ cups strawberries, cleaned, and sliced
2 tablespoons coconut amino or tamari
1 cup almonds or hazelnuts, chopped or sliced, and toasted
⅔ cup olive oil
4 tablespoons raw local honey
⅓ cup fresh orange juice
3 tablespoons fresh lemon juice
½ teaspoon natural salt
1 tablespoon poppy seeds
2 teaspoons dry mustard

METHOD:

Combine arugula and strawberries in a mixing bowl.

Place olive oil, honey, orange juice, lemon juice, salt, poppy seeds, and mustard in a small jar, screw lid securely on the jar, and shake to combine. Taste dressing and adjust seasonings as necessary.

When ready to serve, add desired amount of dressing to greens and toss to combine.

Add toasted nuts to salad bowl or use as a topping if serving individual salads.

CHEF NOTES AND VARIATIONS:

Substitute arugula with mixed salad greens, watercress, spinach, Bibb lettuce, or your favorite salad green combination.

Pairing Guide:
Goat-cheese feta
Snap peas
Grilled shrimp or smoked salmon
Tempeh croutons

Notes:

Salads, Sides, and More

Lentil Salad with Sun-Gold Tomato

Quinoa and Marinated Zucchini Salad

Sesame Broccoli Salad

Crunchy Vegetable and Apple Slaw

Roasted Winter Squash Casserole with Spinach "Ricotta"

Broccoli-Almond Pan Fritters

Stuffed Portobello Pizza Mushrooms

Golden Roasted Cauliflower with Lemon Caper Dressing

LENTIL SALAD WITH SUN-GOLD TOMATO

Small French lentils, or Le Puy, have a velvety texture but retain their shape when cooked. Lentils are smaller, cook more quickly, and are easier to digest than beans.

Servings: 6 to 8

INGREDIENTS:

2 cups French lentils, washed (pick out any debris or small stones)
2 bay leaves
½ pint sun-gold tomato or cherry tomato varieties
1 bunch arugula or watercress
¼ cup red onion, finely minced
1 cup green beans, blanched and cut into small pieces
2 tablespoons chives, minced
3 tablespoons tamari or coconut aminos
1 tablespoon Dijon mustard
⅓ cup olive oil
2 tablespoons organic cider vinegar

METHOD:

Wash and drain lentils, place in pot with bay leaves, and cover with water. Bring lentils to a boil, lower flame, and simmer uncovered until they are soft and firm, about thirty-five minutes. Drain and rinse, remove bay leaves, and place lentils in a bowl.

While lentils are cooking, prepare the vegetables and dressing.

Place tamari, mustard, olive oil, and vinegar in a small jar, secure lid tightly, and shake vigorously to combine. Pour dressing over warm lentils and toss gently.

When lentils have cooled slightly, add sun-gold tomato, greens, green beans, and chives. Stir to combine. Taste and adjust seasoning as needed.

Chef Notes and Variations:

Substitute sun-gold tomato with other seasonal tomatoes, cut into medium-sized dice, and include all of the juice.

Add in extra fresh herbs—parsley and thyme are delicious.

If you are making this in advance, stir in the watercress or arugula right before serving.

PAIRING GUIDE:
Warm sourdough bread, pita bread, or your favorite gluten free bread
Pumpkin Seed Pesto
Grilled, sliced chicken breast
Half of a baked acorn squash
Half of an avocado

NOTES:

QUINOA AND MARINATED ZUCCHINI SALAD

This simple, refreshing summer salad is tasty by itself or as a topper for greens or arugula.

Servings: 6 to 8

INGREDIENTS:

1 cup quinoa, washed thoroughly and rinsed through fine-mesh strainer
1 pound yellow and green zucchini squash
1 teaspoon sea salt or Himalayan pink salt
¼ cup mixed Greek olives, pitted and chopped
½ cup red sweet peppers, medium diced
3 scallions, green and white parts, minced
2 tablespoons extra-virgin olive oil
4 tablespoons fresh lemon juice
1 handful basil leaves, chopped
Salt and pepper to taste

METHOD:

Bring a four-quart pot of water to a boil. Gently pour quinoa into boiling water, turn down to a simmer, and cook for sixteen minutes.

Drain and rinse quinoa, and place in a large mixing bowl.

Trim end from squash and slice into paper-thin rounds with a sharp knife or mandolin slicer. Place sliced squash into a strainer, and toss with 1-teaspoon salt. Drain squash for twenty minutes. Squash will soften and excess water will drain out; pat squash dry with paper towels.

Add squash, olives, red peppers, scallions, olive oil, and basil to quinoa.

Toss all of the salad ingredients to combine thoroughly.

Taste salad and add fresh ground pepper and extra salt if needed.

Store salad in the refrigerator until ready to serve.

CHEF NOTES AND VARIATIONS:

Grain salads soak up the dressing when stored. Taste salad before serving, and refresh it if necessary with an extra dash of olive oil and more lemon. Substitute fresh chopped basil with fresh cilantro.

PAIRING GUIDE:

Bibb lettuce cups or romaine leaves
Pita bread and roasted cherry tomatoes
Black beans or chickpeas
Served in half of an avocado, or cucumber halves with seeds scooped out

NOTES:

Sesame Broccoli Salad

Servings: 6 to 8

Ingredients:
1 head broccoli
3 carrots, trimmed and cleaned
4 scallions, thinly sliced
1 handful fresh cilantro, coarsely chopped
1 teaspoon fresh ginger, grated
3 tablespoons extra-virgin olive oil
2 tablespoons coconut aminos
1 lime, juiced
1 teaspoon toasted sesame oil
1 tablespoon sesame seeds, toasted

Method:
Remove stalks from broccoli florets. Place broccoli in bowl or food processor fitted with S-shaped blade and pulse eight to ten times until coarsely chopped.

Place chopped broccoli in a bowl.

Peel broccoli stalks. Grate broccoli stalks and carrots with grating disc in food processor.

Place in bowl with broccoli, add scallions and cilantro, and toss to combine.

Combine ginger, olive oil, coconut aminos, lime juice, and sesame oil in a small bowl.

Pour dressing over broccoli, and toss with toasted sesame seeds.

Serve broccoli salad as is or refrigerate until ready to serve.

Chef Notes and Variations:
Substitute cilantro with parsley or fresh chives.

PAIRING GUIDE:
Shredded chicken or beef
Your favorite grain or vegetable burger
Rice noodles or quinoa and toasted sesame seeds
Seasonal salad greens
Black beans or chickpeas
Grilled marinated tempeh

NOTES:

CRUNCHY VEGETABLE AND APPLE SLAW

Raw vegetable slaws are a good swap for the traditional leafy green salad. Cabbage is widely available year round and is a good source of calcium, magnesium, fiber, and vitamin C.

Servings: 4 to 6

INGREDIENTS:

½ head cabbage (red, green, or savory), very thinly sliced
2 Granny Smith apples or other tart apple variety, thinly sliced
3 carrots, trimmed, scrubbed, and grated or thinly sliced
½ package crunchy sprouts (lentils, peas, sunflowers, etc.)
¼ cup red onion, thinly sliced
¼ cup almonds, slivered and toasted
¼ cup cilantro, chopped
1 tablespoon Dijon mustard
6 tablespoons raw organic cider vinegar
½ cup olive oil
1 to 2 tablespoons maple syrup or raw honey
Salt and pepper to taste

METHOD:

Place cabbage, apples, carrots, sprouts, red onion, almonds, and cilantro in a mixing bowl.

In a small bowl, mix together mustard, cider vinegar, olive oil, and maple syrup.

Pour dressing over cabbage slaw, and toss to combine. Taste and add salt and pepper as needed.

If you are not eating the salad right away, add nuts right before serving so they remain crunchy.

Chef Notes and Variations:
Substitute sprout mix with other seasonal vegetables, such as radishes, kohlrabi, or celery.
Substitute cilantro with fresh mint and chives.

Pairing Guide:
Broccoli Almond fritters
Shredded chicken
Rice-paper wrappers
Black beans, taco shells, and shredded dairy or nondairy cheese
Mango and turkey or grass-fed beef burger

Notes:

ROASTED WINTER SQUASH CASSEROLE WITH SPINACH "RICOTTA"

Casseroles are a cold-weather companion. They can go from the oven to the table and are bubbling and fragrant, with a crispy topping. They taste even better the next day.

Servings: 4 to 6

INGREDIENTS:

3 pounds butternut squash, peeled, seeds removed, medium diced
2 tablespoons coconut oil or olive oil
2 cloves garlic
1 large sweet onion, peeled, small diced
½ teaspoon chili powder
½ teaspoon natural salt

CASHEW RICOTTA:

1 cup cashews, soaked for at least two hours
1 clove garlic, peeled
1 lemon, juiced
¼ cup nutritional yeast
2 tablespoons extra virgin olive oil
1 teaspoon natural salt
⅓ to ½ cup water
1 handful parsley leaves
2 handfuls spinach leaves
½ cup bread crumbs, gluten-free

METHOD:

Warm a small sauté pan over medium heat, and add oil. Sauté garlic and onions for two to three minutes, until softened.

Place diced butternut squash in a bowl, and toss with sautéed garlic and onions. Add chili powder and salt; stir.

Place butternut squash in a 9-inch by 13-inch greased casserole dish.

Drain soaked cashew nuts and place in food processor fitted with an S-shaped blade.

Add garlic, lemon juice, nutritional yeast, olive oil, salt, and water. Process until almost smooth. Add water a little at a time to get desired consistency.

Add parsley and spinach, and pulse a few times until the mixture is chopped but not pureed.

Place dollops of cashew ricotta in casserole dish in between butternut squash. Sprinkle bread crumbs over the top.

Cover casserole, and bake for thirty-five to forty minutes, until the squash is soft.

Uncover casserole, and cook for an additional fifteen minutes to brown the top.

CHEF NOTES AND VARIATIONS:
Substitute butternut squash with sweet potato.

PAIRING GUIDE:
Roasted Winter Squash Casserole + Salad greens and Italian herb vinaigrette
Oven-roasted cherry tomatoes
Simple sautéed greens
Baked or steamed fish

NOTES:

Broccoli-Almond Pan Fritters

Servings: 6

Ingredients:
1½ pounds broccoli, washed
½ cup onion
3 cloves garlic
¾ cup almond flour or finely ground almonds
½ cup garbanzo bean flour
1 teaspoon salt
1 teaspoon cumin, ground
1 tablespoon olive oil
2 tablespoons golden flaxseeds, ground
2 tablespoons water
Coconut oil

Method:
Cut stems off broccoli, peel stems, and cut into chunks.

Process broccoli florets and stems in food processor fitted with an S-shaped blade in two batches until coarsely chopped. Place broccoli in a large mixing bowl.

Process onions and garlic in food processor until coarsely chopped. Add to broccoli.

Add almond flour, garbanzo bean flour, salt, cumin, olive oil, and mix.

In a small bowl, mix ground flaxseeds and water; let rest for three to five minutes until water is absorbed.

Add ground flaxseed mixture to broccoli mixture. Mix ingredients with hands until everything is thoroughly combined and sticks together.

Form broccoli mixture into ten patties.

Heat sauté pan over medium heat, and add 1 tablespoon of coconut oil.

Place three to four fritters in pan at a time; do not overcrowd the pan. Cook fritters for three to four minutes on each side until golden brown and crispy.

Cook remaining fritters and place on a serving plate to keep warm.

Serve fritters as is or with additional toppings and condiments.

CHEF NOTES AND VARIATIONS:

Serve broccoli fritters with pickled red onions, pesto, lettuce, tomato, or avocado slices.

To reheat, place fritters on sheet pan and bake in 350-degree oven for fifteen to twenty minutes until crispy and hot.

Make mini-sized fritters and serve as an appetizer or a salad topping.

PAIRING GUIDE:

Oven-roasted cherry tomatoes

Pumpkin-seed pesto

Salad greens

Broccoli Almond Pan Fritters + Spicy pickled red onion

Crunchy vegetable apple slaw

NOTES:

STUFFED PORTOBELLO PIZZA MUSHROOMS

Portobello mushroom caps make the perfect container to fill and bake. Coat the inside of the mushroom cap with your favorite tomato sauce and top with cheese.

Servings: 5

INGREDIENTS:

2 tablespoons olive oil
¾ cup onion, minced
3 cloves garlic, peeled
2 eggplants (about 5 cups), peeled and cut into small pieces
1 Portobello mushroom cap, stem removed, minced
5 Portobello mushroom caps, stems removed, cleaned
½ teaspoon natural salt
½ teaspoon dried basil
½ teaspoon dried oregano
1¼ cup tomato sauce
8 ounces dairy-free mozzarella-style cheese or fresh mozzarella
½ cup bread crumbs, dry
¼ cup parsley leaves, chopped
2 tablespoons nutritional yeast or parmesan cheese, grated

METHOD:

Preheat oven to 350 degrees.
Heat 1 tablespoon of olive oil over medium heat in sauté pan. Add onions and garlic, and sauté for two to three minutes until softened.
Add eggplant and a dash of salt, and sauté for a few minutes until softened.
Sauté minced mushroom, and season with salt, basil, and oregano.
Place sautéed vegetables in a bowl; let cool slightly.
Drizzle remaining olive oil in bottom of roasting pan, and add five mushroom caps.

Put 2 tablespoons of tomato sauce in each mushroom cap, and spread out to cover inside of cap.

Slice mozzarella cheese, and place half the cheese slices on top of tomato sauce.

Dice remaining cheese and mix into eggplant filling. Add bread crumbs and parsley, and stir to combine.

Place filling into mushroom caps, dividing evenly between each.

Sprinkle tops of mushrooms with nutritional yeast, and bake for thirty minutes until hot.

Chef Notes and Variations:

Substitute eggplant with green or yellow summer squash.

Pairing Guide:

Coconut creamed spinach

Simple sautéed greens

Wilted spinach and spicy green salad

Local salad greens and Italian herb vinaigrette

Notes:

Golden Roasted Cauliflower with Lemon Caper Dressing

Turmeric root, dried and ground into a powder, is an essential pantry ingredient. This spice has many health benefits, including antibacterial properties. In addition, it provides an excellent source of beta carotene, which aids digestion. Turmeric lends a gorgeous golden color to foods.

Servings: 4 to 6 (as a side dish)

Ingredients:

1 cauliflower, large, with core removed and divided into florets
¾ teaspoon turmeric, ground
2 tablespoons coconut oil
½ teaspoon garlic powder
1 medium red onion or sweet onion, sliced
3 tablespoons fresh lemon juice, fresh
2 tablespoons extra-virgin olive oil
1½ tablespoons small capers, drained
1 handful parsley, chopped
A pinch of natural salt

Method:

Preheat oven to 400 degrees.
Place cauliflower florets, turmeric, salt, coconut oil, garlic powder, and red onion in a bowl. Toss to combine, thoroughly coating cauliflower with oil and spices.
Place seasoned cauliflower on sheet pan lined with parchment paper.
Roast cauliflower in oven for thirty-five to forty minutes until golden and crispy. Turn cauliflower over during cooking so all sides brown.
In a small bowl, combine lemon juice, olive oil, parsley, capers, and salt.
Toss dressing with warm roasted cauliflower.
Serve warm or at room temperature.

CHEF NOTES AND VARIATIONS:
Substitute capers for sliced Greek olives or Kalamata olives

PAIRING GUIDE:
Zucchini noodles made with spiralizer
Roasted chickpeas
Simple sautéed greens
Linguini or rice noodles
Pan-seared salmon or shrimp
Sesame crusted salmon

NOTES:

Sweet Treats

Raw Chocolate Truffles

Cherry Almond Bars

Cashew Coconut Cream with Berries

RAW CHOCOLATE TRUFFLES

This is a yummy, nut-free, chocolate treat. Hemp seeds have a powerful nutritional profile; they are a good source of essential fatty acids, protein, and magnesium and high in fiber.

Servings: 2-3 dozen

INGREDIENTS:
12 Medjool dates, pitted and cut into small pieces
½ cup rolled oats
1½ cups hemp seeds
⅓ cup raw cacao powder or unsweetened cocoa powder
1 teaspoon vanilla extract
A pinch of natural salt
2 tablespoons raw honey or maple syrup
2 tablespoons coconut oil
½ cup mini chocolate chips (dairy-free and gluten-free)

METHOD:
Place oats and hemp seeds in food processor fitted with an S-shaped blade, and pulse ingredients until finely ground.
Add dates to food processor, and pulse until combined.
Add cacao powder, vanilla, salt, honey, and coconut oil. Blend until mixture comes together and forms a ball.
Check consistency; it should be slightly sticky.
Remove mixture from food processor, and place in a bowl.
Place mini chocolate chips into a small bowl.
Form mixture into small, walnut-sized balls. Roll balls into mini chocolate chips, gently pressing to adhere to truffle. Place truffles in small paper cups on a pan and refrigerate until ready to serve; they will firm up when chilled.

Serve truffles chilled or at room temperature, and garnish tray with fresh berries.

NOTES:

CHERRY ALMOND BARS

Prepare these easy dessert or snack bars using simple pantry ingredients. When chilled, wrap individually for a nutritious snack or lunchbox treat.

Servings: 16 to 20

INGREDIENTS:
1½ cups almonds or walnuts
½ teaspoon natural salt
½ cup coconut flour
½ cup organic brown sugar, xylitol, or coconut sugar
1 teaspoon cinnamon, ground
½ cup coconut oil or organic butter
2 tablespoons water
2 cups organic cherry jam, made with all fruit and no added sweeteners

METHOD:
Preheat oven to 350 degrees.
Lightly grease 8-inch-by-8-inch pan with a little coconut oil or butter.
Place nuts, salt, coconut flour, sugar, and cinnamon in a food processor fitted with an S-shaped blade. Process ingredients until combined and nuts are finely chopped.
Add coconut oil and water, and pulse to combine. Mixture should be moist.
Sprinkle two cups of crust mixture evenly into the bottom of greased pan. Use your fingertips to gently press down the dough, making sure the corners of pan are covered.
Spread cherry jam evenly over the crust with a spatula.
Crumble the remaining crust over the top of the jam, and gently press down so crumbs adhere.
Bake for thirty minutes or until lightly browned. Let cool completely before cutting into squares.
Store in the refrigerator.

CHEF NOTES AND VARIATIONS:

Substitute cherry jam with your favorite—strawberry, blueberry, or another—or with mixed fruit.

CASHEW COCONUT CRÈME SAUCE

Subtly sweet and high in protein, cashews are a good base for sweet and savory sauces. Pair this simple sauce with fresh seasonal berries or warm, broiled peach, plum or apricot sprinkled with cinnamon and lemon juice.

Servings: 2 cups

INGREDIENTS:

1 cup raw cashew nuts
½ cup nondairy milk
½ cup coconut milk
1 tablespoon sweetener of your choice
1 vanilla bean, split in half
A pinch of natural salt

METHOD:

Place cashew nuts in a bowl or jar and cover with water; seal top with foil or other wrap. Soak in refrigerator overnight. Drain nuts and discard water.

Place nondairy milk and coconut milk in small saucepan with vanilla bean. Bring liquid to a boil, turn heat down to a simmer, and cook for fifteen minutes. Remove vanilla bean from liquid. Scrape out the insides of vanilla bean pod with a small knife, and add back to liquid.

Place nuts, vanilla milk, sweetener, and a pinch of salt into blender, and combine until very smooth and creamy. Add more liquid if needed to achieve desired consistency.

Serve sauce warm or chilled.

CHEF NOTES AND VARIATIONS:

Substitute cashew nuts with whole raw almonds; soak overnight and remove skins before using.

Substitute vanilla bean with one-teaspoon vanilla extract.

Add one to two tablespoons raw cacao powder and ½ teaspoon coffee extract for a mocha crème.

NOTES:

How Can I Help?

Are you looking for more inspiration and support to live a healthier life? Contact me through my website, www.anaturalchef.com. Here you will find recipes, easy lifestyle tips, and other resources.

Please reach out if you are looking for personalized support, have any questions, or want to set up a FREE thirty-minute goal-setting session.

Follow Cathy on Facebook at
https://www.facebook.com/A-Natural-Chef-1184736228218652/timeline/?ref=hl

Resources

Natural Gourmet Institute, www.naturalgourmetinstitute.com

Institute for Integrative Nutrition, www.integrativenutrition.com

Institute for the Psychology of Eating, www.psychologyofeating.com

Breathing Center: Holistic Health Improvement, www.breathingcenter.com

Environmental Working Group, www.ewg.org (consumer guides to healthy eating, cleaning product, skin care, etc.).

Saladmaster, www.saladmaster.com (featuring healthy cookware made in the United States).

About the Author

SINCE HER EARLY twenties, Cathy has been a student of healthy cooking and lifestyle practices.

She is a professionally trained chef and culinary translator who is focused on educating clients on how to adopt healthier eating and lifestyle habits. She is also a certified integrative nutrition coach, eating psychology coach, and breathing normalization specialist.

In 1996 Cathy's business, A Natural Chef, was born, offering her clients personal chef services and health and nutrition coaching programs. Cathy also works as a professional recipe developer for an international cookware company.

Cathy received her culinary training at the Natural Gourmet Institute in New York City and at the State University of New York at Cobleskill College. Cathy furthered her training at the Institute for Integrative Nutrition, where she trained in more than one hundred dietary theories and practical lifestyle-coaching methods. She studied with the world's top health and nutrition experts, including Joshua Rosenthal, David Wolfe, Marc David, Annemarie Colbin, Dr. Andrew Weil, Geneen Roth, Joel Fuhrman, and others.

Cathy is accredited by the American Association of Drugless Practitioners and received additional certification from Columbia University.

Cathy is a happily married, busy mom of two beautiful daughters. In her free time, she enjoys hiking in the exquisite Hudson Valley, reading cookbooks and health and nutrition books, spending time with family, friends, and gardening.